[1] MODEL OF THE WHALER "DEBORAH GIFFORD," OF NEW BEDFORD.
From a photograph of the model in the Old Dartmouth Historical Society, New Bedford.

WHALE SHIPS
AND
WHALING

A Pictorial History

by

GEORGE FRANCIS DOW

DOVER PUBLICATIONS, INC.
New York

This Dover edition, first published in 1985, is an unabridged republication of the work first published by The Marine Research Society, Salem, Mass., in 1925. In the original edition the illustrations were printed on one side of the page only. In this edition they are printed on both sides, thereby reducing the number of pages in the work. No material from the first edition has been omitted here.

Library of Congress Cataloging in Publication Data

Dow, George Francis, 1868–1936.
  Whale ships and whaling.

  Reprint. Originally published: Salem, Mass. : Marine Research Society, 1925. (Publication no. 10 of the Marine Research Society)
  Includes index.
  1. Whaling—New England—History—Pictorial works. 2. Whaling ships—New England—History—Pictorial works. I. Title. II. Series: Publication . . . of the Marine Research Society; no. 10.
SH383.2.D69 1985   639'.28'0222   84-25921
ISBN-13: 978-0-486-24808-0
ISBN-10: 0-486-24808-9

Manufactured in the United States by RR Donnelley
24808909   2015
www.doverpublications.com

PREFACE

THE keen interest in whale ships and whaling that exists at the present time has led to the production of this volume. Many books have been written descriptive of the industry and of the lives and adventures of whalemen but, so far as known, no effort has ever been made to present a comprehensive pictorial survey showing the whale ships of all periods. Aside from the modern use of the whaling gun, the methods followed in killing the quarry have changed but little during historic times; but ships have changed with the centuries and the following illustrations will be found to have preserved a record of whalers and whaling valuable alike to those who would study the evolution of a dying industry and also to the builder and collector of models of these ships.

As a suitable background for this pictorial history of whaling, especially when viewed by American eyes, it has seemed fitting to include some account of the whale fishery in colonial New England. Public archives and contemporaneous newspaper accounts have been drawn upon as well as the gatherings of local historians; but the principal source of information has been the painstaking survey of the industry made by the late Alexander Starbuck and published in the "Report of the United States Commission of Fish and Fisheries for the year 1875-1876."

The nucleus from which the following collection of illustrations has grown was found in the "Allan Forbes Collection of Whaling Pictures," a wonderful gathering of all kinds of material relating in any way to the subject. Mr. Forbes generously made available the resources of this great collection—so large in its compass that the difficulty has been to decide what not to use. Mr. A. G. H. Macpherson of Alverstoke, Hants, England, at some personal inconvenience, threw open the resources of his remarkable collection of marine and naval prints, probably the largest in the world, and caused photographs to be made of rare prints and early engravings relating to the field of European whaling; and Captain Harry Parker, the well-known London dealer in naval prints, most generously placed his selected gatherings at our command.

Mr. Frank Wood, the curator of the Bourne Whaling Museum at New Bedford, Mass., has aided the work in every way and finally consented to write the Introduction to the volume. Colonel E. H. R. Green of New Bedford, with a generous spirit of coöperation, had many photographs made of the old-time whaler *Charles W. Morgan,* purchased by him, and many of these photographs are here reproduced. Thanks are also due to the officials of the Peabody Museum of Salem; to Miss Sarah L. Dunfee, Curator of the Marine Museum, Massachusetts Institute of Technology; and to all others who may have aided in any way in the production of this volume.

CONTENTS

INTRODUCTION

THERE was a time, within the memory of a great many citizens of New Bedford, when the wharves of the city were swarmed with ships and barks, whose hundreds of masts fringed the sky-line like the bayonets of a great army marshalled in battle array. Today we look in vain for one of those grimy, storm-stained square-riggers. Cotton mills, with hovering clouds of smoke, now greet the eye as it looks along the water-front. The clack of looms and the whirr of spindles greet the ear. Only in one way does the past come back to us and that way, curiously enough, is through the sense of smell. The tiers of barrels of whale oil, covered with sea weed, as was the custom, formerly occupied much space on the wharves and more or less of the oil would seep out through the cracks in the barrels, and permeate the timbers and the soil on the wharves. The odor is still strong. Like the odor of the mignonette shut between the leaves of a favorite old book, it recalls a past.

And we have under consideration a past that is worth recalling. Communities like Nantucket, New Bedford and New London grew to prominence and waxed prosperous on whaling and its subsidiary occupations alone. Bold journeys were made to all parts of the ocean, and not a little of the exploration done in the last century may be attributed to the whalemen. And these whalemen formed, in a sense, a race apart. In towns where whaling was an exclusive industry, boys were born with the fever of the sea in their veins. Distant journeys to quasi-legendary lands, where strange folk lived; dangers of storms and of uncharted seas, of merciless ice-floes in the Arctic, of the sickly heat in the equatorial Pacific; tremendous conflicts with the largest and most powerful creature known on this globe—all the mystery, the glamor and the romance of whaling fed the flames of boyish imagination and desire. As youngsters, they listened to the tales of their elders, gazed with wonder at the queer men—the "Queequegs" that the ships often brought home. And they would watch the vessels leaving the harbor, as the proud masses of canvass would fade away at the horizon. And they would see them return, deep in the water with a lucky catch. But between the departure and the return, in watery realms far, far beyond the horizon, what brave glory there must be!

But soon the imaginative boy became the practical man. Folk seemed to mature early in those days, back in the '40s and '50s, and crew lists show many a greenhand in his 'teens and many a master in his twenties. We often hear the saying, "A person never went whaling more than once." But this statement is true only of those young men who were lured to the whaling ports from up-country. The boys of the ports themselves, born and bred to the sea, if they answered to the call once, generally made whaling their career and rose through the ranks. If such young men made but one voyage, they considered it not as time lost, but as an important part of their education, fitting them for a better understanding of their life-work on shore, in counting-houses, in ship-owners' offices, in any of the smaller businesses that were nourished by whaling.

The hardships that they endured, the bravery that they were forced to display, the ennui they were taught to master, made of the whalemen a dauntless, strong-charactered race of men. We do not find the type today except in individual cases.

Ofttimes we hear, too, that the whaleships were floating hells, and it is true that there were many deplorable abuses connected with whaling. But let us look for a moment at the brighter side. The whalemen of course had to put up with many of the disagreeable features of any life at sea, but, on the other hand, their work was not so exacting as the work on board a merchantman. In the latter case, the seamen were forced to climb the rigging a dozen or so times a day to furl some sail, to set another or to reef, for every little change in wind demanded a change in sail to maintain the highest speed possible. But the whaler never was concerned with speed; she sailed idly along—a whale might be found in one place as easily as in another. Then, too, the whaler was never kept as spic and span as a merchantman; there was not the continual holystoning for the men. And a witness to this phase of the whaleman's existence, a witness to his leisure, exists in the large amount of scrimshaw work made from whales' teeth and bone to carry home as gifts.

Of course it goes without saying that when a whale was sighted, the whalemen were in for a hard job, a harder job than the uninitiated could ever appreciate. The chase, the capture, the cutting-in, the trying-out were dangerous and inordinately wearisome. But the chase and the capture, too, had their better sides. The love of a princely sport thrilled the whalemen when the cry of "blows" came from aloft. As trout-fishermen feel when they sense the first little nibble, the herald of joyful battle, so did the whalemen feel, when the harpoon buried itself into the giant whale — when the iron "tuk" and the chase was on and human ingenuity and courage and perseverance must be strained to their very limits. Like the trout-fishermen, indeed, but how far greater the danger, how far more difficult the art, how far more glorious the thrill!

FRANK WOOD.
Curator of the Bourne Whaling Museum
New Bedford, Mass.

New Bedford,
July 31, 1925.

THE WHALE FISHERY IN
COLONIAL NEW ENGLAND

THE WHALE FISHERY IN
COLONIAL NEW ENGLAND

MANY years before the first settlements were made in New England, fishing vessels from overseas frequented the coast. It was fully a century before the "Mayflower" sailed into Plymouth harbor, when French fishermen from St. Malo, Dieppe and Honfleur were catching cod on the banks off Newfoundland. English whale ships went to Cape Breton in the year 1593 and although they returned without having made any captures, yet they discovered on an island some eight hundred whale fins left by a Biscay ship that had been there three years earlier.

Samuel de Champlain, the navigator and founder of the French settlements in North America, on returning to France from his second voyage, sailed from the mouth of the St. Lawrence River on August 18th, 1610, and when "about half way across, we encountered a whale, which was asleep. The vessel, passing over him, awakening him betimes, made a great hole in him near the tail, without damaging our vessel; but he threw out an abundance of blood.

"It has seemed to me not out of place to give here a brief description of the mode of catching whales, which many have not witnessed, and suppose that they are shot, owing to the false assertions about the matter made to them in their ignorance by impostors, and on account of which such ideas have often been obstinately maintained in my presence.

"Those, then, most skillful in this fishery are the Basques, who, for the purpose of engaging in it, take their vessels to a place of security, and near where they think whales are plenty. Then they equip several shallops manned by competent men and provided with hawsers, small ropes made of the best hemp to be found, at least a hundred and fifty fathoms long. They are also provided with many halberds of the length of a short pike, whose iron is six inches broad; others are from a foot and a half to two feet long, and very sharp. Each shallop has a harpooner, the most agile and adroit man they have, whose pay is next highest to that of the masters, his position being the most dangerous one. This shallop being outside of the port, the men look in all quarters for a whale, tacking about in all directions. But, if they see nothing, they return to shore and ascend the highest point they can find, and from which they can get the most extensive view. Here they station a man on the lookout. They are aided in catching sight of a whale by his size and the water he spouts through his blow-holes, which is more than a puncheon at a time and two lances high. From the amount of this water, they estimate how much oil he will yield. From some they get as many as one hundred and twenty puncheons, and from others less. Having caught sight of this monstrous fish, they hasten to embark in their shallops, and by rowing or sailing they advance until they are upon him.

"Seeing him under water, the harpooner goes at once to the prow of the shallop with his harpoon, an iron two feet long and half a foot wide at the lower part, and attached to a stick as long as a small pike, in the middle of which is a hole to which the hawser is made fast. The harpooner, watching his time, throws his harpoon at the whale, which enters him well forward. As soon as he finds himself wounded, the whale goes down, and if by chance turning about, as he does sometimes, his tail strikes the shallop, it breaks it like glass. This is the only risk they run of being killed in harpooning. As soon as they have thrown the harpoon into him, they let the hawser run until the whale reaches the bottom; but sometimes he does not go straight to the bottom, when he drags the shallop eight or nine leagues or more, going as swiftly as a horse. Very often they are obliged to cut their hawser, for fear that the whale will take them under water. But, when he goes straight to the bottom, he rests there awhile, and then returns quietly to the surface, the men taking aboard again the hawser as he rises. When he comes to the top, two or three shallops are stationed around with halberds, with which they give him several blows. Finding himself struck, the whale goes down again, leaving a trail of blood and grows weak to such an extent that he has no longer any strength nor energy, and returning to the surface is finally killed. When dead he does not go down again. Fastening stout ropes to him, they drag him ashore to their headquarters, the place where they try out the fat of the whale to obtain his oil. This is the way whales are taken, and not by cannon-shots, which many suppose, as I have stated above."[1]

The date of the coming of the first ship sent out on a whaling venture to New England is not known, but it may have been in April, 1614, when Capt. John Smith arrived at Monhegan, off the coast of Maine, with two ships from London.

"Our plot was there to take Whales, for which we had one *Samuel Cramton*, and divers others expert in the faculty. . . . We found this Whale-fishing a costly conclusion; we saw many and spent much time in chasing them, but could not kill any. They being a kind of *Tubartes*, and not the whale that yields Fins and Oils as we expected."[2]

Elsewhere he mentions that whales were common off the New England coast and when he arrived in London on July 18, 1614, after an absence of less than six months, his ship brought back furs, train oil (whale oil) and cor-fish (dried cod fish) the best of which sold at £5. the hundred.

When the "Mayflower" came to anchor at Cape Cod, in December, 1620, the Pilgrims debated mightily whether they should remain there or find a settlement at Agawam, now Ips-

[1] *Voyages of Samuel de Champlain*, New York, 1907, pp. 190, 191.
[2] Smith, *Generall Historie of Virginia, New England and the Summer Isles*, London, 1624.

wich, and one of the arguments advanced for remaining at Cape
Cod was that "it was a place of profitable fishing, for large whales
of the best kind for oil and bone came daily alongside and played
about the ship. The master and his mate, and others experi-
enced in fishing, preferred it to the Greenland whale fishery and
asserted that were they provided with the proper implements,
£ 300. or £400. worth of oil might be obtained.""

The Royal Charter under which the first settlements were
made in the Massachusetts Bay, guaranteed to the colonists
their rights to unrestricted fishing, in fact, it was a colony of
fishermen that was at first contemplated. The Province Charter
of 1691 also confirmed the rights of the colonists to "free Liber-
tie of Fishing . . . in the Seas thereunto adjoyning and of all
Fishes Royall Fishes Whales Balene Sturgeon and other Fishes
of what kind or nature soever."

At that time whales undoubtedly were very numerous along
the New England coast and also in deep water. When the Rev.
Francis Higginson, the first minister at Salem, published his
New Englands Plantation (London, 1630), he wrote of seeing
a "great store of Whales and Grampusse" while on the voyage
over, and five years later, when Rev. Richard Mather came over
and became the minister at Dorchester, he wrote of seeing near
the coast "mighty whales spewing up water in the air, like the
smoke of a chimney, and making the sea about them white and
hoary, as is said in Job, of such incredible bigness that I will
never wonder that the body of Jonas could be in the belly of a
whale."[4]

A still earlier voyager along the coast was Capt. George Way-
mouth, who sailed from Dartmouth, March 15, 1605, intending
to visit the regions south of Cape Cod, but meeting with con-
trary winds after making his landfall, he bore away to the east-

---

[3] Thatcher, *History of Plymouth*, p. 21. See also Morton, *New England's Memorial*,
p. 42.
[4] Young, *Chronicles of the First Planters of the Colony of Massachusetts Bay*, Boston,
1845.

ward and anchored on the north side of the island of Monhegan off the coast of Maine. After exploring the nearby coast he sailed for England taking with him five Indians from the region of the Kennebec river. His narrative was published the same year and in it he describes the manner in which the Kennebec Indians captured the whale.

"One especial thing is their manner of killing the whale, which they call powdawe; and will describe his form: how he bloweth up the water; and that he is twelve fathoms long; and that they go in company of their king with a multitude of boats, and strike him with a bone made in fashion of a harping iron fastened to a rope, which they make great and strong of the bark of trees, which they vear out after him; then all their boats come about him, and as he riseth above water, with their arrows they shoot him to death: when they have killed him and dragged him to shore, they call all their chief lords together and sing a song of joy; and those chief lords, whom they call Sagamores, divide the spoil, and give to every man a share, which pieces so distributed, they hang up about their houses for provision; and when they boil them, they blow off the fat, and put to their pease, maize, and other pulse which they eat."[5]

Samuel Purchas in his *Pilgrimage* describes in some detail how the English whalers pursued the whale at this time. Writing in 1612 he remarks: "I might here recreate your wearied eyes with a hunting spectacle of the greatest chase which Nature yieldeth: I mean the killing of a whale. When they espy him on the top of the water (which he is forced to for to take breath), they row toward him in a shallop, in which the harpooner stands ready with both his hands to dart his harping iron, to which is fastened a line of such length that the whale (which suddenly feeling himself hurt, sinketh to the bottom) may carry it down with him, being before fitted that the shallop be not therewith endangered; coming up again, they strike him with lances made

[5] *Mass. Hist. Soc. Colls.* 3d series, Vol. VIII.

for that purpose, about twelve feet long, the iron eight thereof and the blade eighteen inches—the harping iron principally serving to fasten him to the shallop, and thus they hold him in such pursuit, till after streams of water, and next of blood, cast up into the air and water (as if angry with both elements, which have brought thither such weak hands for his destruction), he at length yieldeth up his slain carcass as meed to the conquerors."[6]

Oils and fats were highly esteemed by our ancestors and occupied an important place in trade. Train oil, so-called, produced from the blubber of the whale, was used not only in the making of leather and for lighting, but also entered largely into the composition of the cargoes of vessels bound for London, Bristol and other English ports. Fish of various kinds were caught in such numbers that they were used as fertilizer in the corn fields, and fish oil became an article of export. In every household the animal fats were carefully preserved and used in the making of soap and candles. While candles made from tallow were in daily use in every home, all well-equipped kitchen fireplaces had their iron "betty lamps," used to light the inside of the pots and kettles in cooking, and other lamps of metal and even glass were used for lighting in prosperous homes. The streets in the larger towns were lighted but feebly. As late as the year 1668, the inhabitants of London, the first and largest city in the Kingdom, were ordered "to hang out candles duly to the accustomed hour, for the peace and safety of the city." It was not until 1716, that householders were directed to "hang out a lamp on every night between the second after the full-moon until the seventh after the new moon, from the hour of six in the evening until eleven."

Whale oil furnished the best light and whalebone, or baleen, the fringed plates through which the right whale sifted its food, was used in clothing and in the arts.

---

[6] *Purchas his Pilgrimage, or Relations of the World . . . in all Ages and Places,* London, 1613.

In the early days whaling was carried on in New England by means of boats from off shore, and most of the captures were made along the south shore of Massachusetts Bay and in the warmer waters south of Cape Cod. As early as 1641 the Great and General Court of Massachusetts "ordered and decreed, That if any ships or other vessels, be it friend or enemy, shall suffer ship-wreck upon our coasts, there shall be no violence or wrong offered to their persons, or goods, but their persons shall be Harboured and Releived, and their goods preserved in safety, till Authority may be certified, and shall take further Order Therein. Also any Whale, or such like great fish cast upon any shore, shall be safely kept or improved where it cannot be kept, by the town or other proprietor of the land, til the Generall Court shall set Order for the same."[7]

The right whale probably was very common along-shore at that time for there are numerous references to drift whales in the seventeenth century records of New England shore towns. These drift whales were prizes for the lucky finders and disputes at once arose as to the relative rights of the Colony and the finder. In 1652, the town of Sandwich, Mass., appointed six men to secure and divide oil-bearing fish that the Indians might cut up within the town limits. They also were to act as agents to receive the oil for the country.[8] Ten years later the town of Eastham voted that a part of every whale cast ashore should be apportioned for the support of the ministry. History fails to relate what may have taken place when a whale was sighted in the breakers during the public exercise on a Sunday morning. From all drift whales the Colony claimed one hogshead or two barrels of oil to be delivered in Boston.

In 1676, Edward Randolph, the British Agent in Boston, wrote home to the Lords of Trade, of the great quantity of whale oil made in the Plymouth Colony and again, in 1688, he wrote:

[7] *Book of the General Lawes and Libertyes concerning the Inhabitants of the Massachusets*, Cambridge, 1660.
[8] Freeman, *Cape Cod*, pp. 50, 51.

"New Plimouth Colony have great profit by whale killing. I believe it will be one of our best returnes, now beaver and peltry fayles us." The same year a memorandum appears in the Colony Archives which embodies the universally recognized law of whalemen that "craft claims the whale." It specifies:

"Furst: if aney persons shall find a Dead Whael on the streem And have the opportunity to toss herr on shoure; then ye owners to alow them twenty shillings; 2ly: if thay cast hur out & secure ye blubber & bone then ye owners to pay them for it 30s. (that is if ye whael ware lickly to be loast;) 3ly, if it proves a floatesom not killed by men then ye Admirall to Doe Thaire in as he shall please;— 4ly; that no persons shall presume to cut up any whael till she be vewed by toe persons not consarned; that so ye Right owners may not be Rongged of such whael or whaels; 5ly, that no whael shall be needlessly or fouellishly lansed behind ye vitall to avoid stroy; 6ly, that each companys harping Iron & Lance be Distinckly marked on ye heads & socketts with a poblick mark: to ye prevention of strife; 7ly, that if a whael or whaells be found & no Iron in them; then thay that lay ye neerest claim to them by thaire strokes & ye natoral markes to have them; 8ly, if 2 or 3 companyes lay equal claimes, then thay equally to shear."[9]

In November, 1690, the Plymouth Colony enacted a law requiring towns to appoint inspectors of whales and the following rules were set forth to govern their work:

"1. All whales killed or wounded & left at sea the killers to repair to the inspectors & give marks, time, place, which shall be recorded.

"2. All whales brought or cast ashore to be viewed by inspector or deputy before being cut & marks & wounds recorded with time & place.

"3. Any person cutting or defacing a whale before being viewed unless necessary shall lose right to it, & pay 10 £ to coun-

9 *Massachusetts Archives*, Vol. 125, leaf 80.

ty, & fish to be seized by inspectors for owner's use. Inspectors to have power to make deputy and allow 6s. per whale.

"4. Those finding a whale a mile from shore not appearing to be killed by man shall be first to secure them, pay 1 hogshead of oyle to ye county for each whale."[10]

An original return made by one of these inspectors of whales is now in the possession of Mr. Lawrence W. Jenkins of Salem, and reads as follows:—

"Decem^r ye 3 1724 I was desired by Obediah Lamson to observe the marks of a whale cut up by him at Duxborough beach which ware as folleth. A short bone with 2 iarnholes one on her rite side about 6 feete abaft her spouts w'h iarn I gug mortal the other about 4 feete back of that & sumthing on the left side of her back boane not mortal and I gudg pricked with a lance one on the rite fin near the joynt. I suposed this fish to be killed 4 or 5 days be fore this date.

"Joshua Soule."

Whaling alongshore began early on Long Island and it is probable that the first organized whale fishing on the coast began there. The town of Southampton, at the eastern end of Long Island, was settled in 1640 by men from Lynn in the Massachusetts Colony, and four years later the town was divided into four wards, with eleven persons in each ward, to care for drift whales that might be cast ashore. Two persons from each ward (selected by lot) were charged with the duty of cutting up the whale, "and every Inhabitant with his child or servant that is above sixteen years of age shall have in the Division of the other part [*i. e.* the part that remained after the cutters had deducted the double share to which by vote they were entitled] an equall proportion provided that such person when y^t falls into his ward a sufficient man to be imployed aboute y^t."[11] In 1645, the town

[10] *Plymouth Colony Records*, VI, pp. 252-3.
[11] Howell, *History of Southampton.*

voted that no man should take or carry away any whale cast ashore within the limits of the town without an order from a magistrate under a penalty of twenty shillings, and anyone finding a whale, on notifying a magistrate should be allowed five shillings. "And y^t is further ordered that yf any shall finde a whale or any peece thereof upon the Lord's day then the aforesaid shillings shall not be due or payable." The historian of Southampton remarks "this last clause, appears to be a very shrewd thrust at 'mooning' on the beach on Sundays."

A few years later it was customary to fit out expeditions of several boats to go whaling along the Long Island coast. These expeditions frequently would be away from home for a week or two and camps on shore would be made at night. Indians were employed in the crews even at that early date, the payment for services usually being made in oil. In 1668, Indian whalemen were paid wages at the rate of three shillings per day. The whaling season was from November 1st to April 1st. There were many complaints from the Indians to the government. In early deeds of the town of Easthampton, Long Island, the Indian grantors were to be allowed the fins and tails of all drift whales; but in the deed of Montauk Island, the Indians and white settlers were to share equally. Easthampton voted in 1651 "that Goodman Mulford shall call out ye Towne by succession to loke out for whales."

A memorandum appears among the papers of the British Secretary of State, under date of 1667, bearing upon affairs in New England, in which he records the fact that the sea was rich in whales near Delaware Bay, but that they were to be found in greatest number about the end of Long Island comparable with the richness of the cod fishery about Nova Scotia.[12]

In 1672, a memorial was presented to the Court at Whitehall, setting forth that the towns of Easthampton, Southampton and Southwold, on Long Island, had "spent much time and paines,

[12] *Cal. State Papers, Colonial Series* (1661-1668), p. 533.

and the greatest part of their Estates, in settling the trade of Whale-fishing in the adjacent seas, having endeavoured it above these twenty years, but could not bring it to any perfection till within these 2 or 3 yeares last past. And it now being a hopefull trade at New Yorke, in America, the Governor and the Dutch there do require ye Petitioners to come under their Patent, and lay very heavy taxes upon them beyond any of his Maties subjects in New England, and will not permit the petitioners to have any deputys in Court, but being chiefe, do impose what Laws they please upon them, and insulting very much over the Petitioners threaten to cut down their timber which is but little they have to make Casks for oyle, altho' the Pet^{rs} purchased their landes of the Lord Sterling's deputy, above 30 yeares since, and have till now been under the Government and Patent of Mr Winthrop, belonging to Conitycut Patent, which lyeth far more convenient for ye Petitioners assistance in the aforesaid Trade."[13]

This memorial seems to indicate that off-shore whaling in boats from the eastern end of Long Island probably began about 1669-1670. A letter written in April, 1669, by Samuel Maverick of Boston, to Col. Richard Nicolls, the first English governor of New York, has an interesting bearing upon this point, showing that about the same time small vessels were being fitted out in Boston to go a-whaling. He writes:

"On ye East end of Long Island there were 12 or 13 whales taken before ye end of March, and what since wee heare not; here are dayly some seen in the very harbour, sometimes within Nutt Island. Out of the Pinnace the other week they struck two, but lost both, the iron broke in one, the other broke the warpe. The Governor hath encouraged some to follow this designe. Two shallops made for itt, but as yett wee doe not heare of any they have gotten."[14] The same year he wrote that twenty whales had been captured that spring.

13 *New York Colonial MSS.* VI, p. 75.
14 *New York Colonial Records*, III, p. 183.

New York already had taken steps to establish a whale fishery for in December, 1652, the Directors of the Dutch West India Company wrote to Governor Stuyvesant at New York: "In regard to the whale fishery we understand that it might be taken in hand during some part of the year. If this could be done with advantage, it would be a very desirable matter, and make the trade there flourish and animate many people to try their good luck in that branch."[15] Three years later the Council of New York "received the request of Hans Jough, soldier and tanner, asking for a tun of train-oil or some of the fat of the whale lately captured."

At the town meeting held at Southampton in the spring of 1672 an ordinance was adopted regulating the employment of Indians in the whale fishery, whereby "whosoever shall Hire an Indyan to go a-whaling, shall not give him for his Hire above one Trucking Cloath Coat, for each whale, he and his Company shall kill, or halfe the Blubber, without the Whale Bone." This was consented to by the Governor who also directed that "the like Rule shall be followed at East Hampton and other Places if they shall finde it practicable amongst them." The Governor also appointed a commission to visit Long Island and make strict inquiries among the English and also Indians concerning alleged abuses in the matter of drift whales.

The inhabitants of Southampton at an early date found it desirable that all agreements "between the English and Indians relating to the killing of whales should be entered in the town books and signed by the parties in the presence of the clerk and certified by him. Boat-whaling was so generally practiced and was considered of so much importance by the whole community, that every man in the town of sufficient ability was obliged to take his turn in watching for whales from some elevated position on the beach, and to sound the alarm on one being seen near the coast."[16]

---

[15] *New York Colonial MSS.*
[16] Howell, *History of Southampton.*

In April, 1668, an agreement was entered on the town records of Easthampton binding certain Indians of Montauket in the sum of £ 10 sterling, to go to sea a-whaling, on account of Jacobus Skallenger and others, beginning on the first of November and ending on the first of April, they engaging "to attend diligently with all opportunities for yᵉ killing of whales or other fish, for yᵉ sum of three shillings a day for every Indian, ye sayd Jacobus Skallenger and partners to furnish all necessarie craft and tackling convenient for yᵉ design."

Laws were enacted governing the operations of these whaling companies. A member of one company finding a dead whale killed by another company was obliged to notify the latter. The finder, however, must be rewarded. If the whale was found at sea, the finders and the killers were to share equally. If irons were found in the whale, they were to be restored to the owners.

As time went on drift whales did not disappear but they became more scarce. As early as 1681, Andros reported that very few whales were driven on shore unless proved to have been struck by the fishermen. When the shores were well watched and boats patrolled the fishing grounds, there were few stranded whales. The boat fishery continued active until well into the eighteenth century. A memorandum kept by widow Martha Smith of St. George's Manor, Long Island, records interesting details of the shore whaling in 1707. In January, "my company" killed a yearling whale that made twenty-seven barrels of oil. On February 4, Indian Harry from his own boat struck a whale but he failed to kill it, and Mrs. Smith's boat was called to assist and the combined force gaining a victory. Mrs. Smith received a third of the oil amounting to four barrels. February 22, "my two boats and my son's and Floyd's boats" killed a yearling that produced thirty-six barrels. Her share was one half. "A school whale" yielded thirty-five barrels. In the month of June Mrs. Smith paid to the authorities in New York £ 15. 15s. as a tithe or tax, it being one twentieth part of her gains for the past season's whaling.[17]

This tax imposed by the Royal Governors was an irritating grievance. Bellomont, in 1700, seized a whale found on the beach bearing the private marks of the person who had killed it and he impressed a man who was employed by the owner, to cut up the carcass. Lord Cornbury gave out that "the whale was a Royal fish," and would not permit whaling without a license. Governor Dongan seized all drift whales and Governor Dudley, in 1705, seized the whales taken by boats "under a Pretence of drift fish" and would not try the question at common law, but decided it in "the Admiralty."

John Hull, the Boston mintmaster who made the "pine tree shillings," was also a merchant and shipowner. His diary shows how the trade in whale oil was conducted. In February, 1671, he records that "the men of Long Island, this winter, made a hundred or two tuns of oil of whales that they there kill." Boston became the commercial port for this industry and it seems probable that Hull was active in introducing the trade. In 1675 he sent his ketch "Sea-flower," Capt. John Harris, to Long Island, and in his "instructions" he ordered the captain to stow his whale oil with great care and to fill all the chinks in the cargo with bone of large size. The vessel was partly loaded in Boston with a miscellaneous cargo, which was to be sold at Long Island or returned by a chance vessel. The captain was to sell the oil and bone in England and then, if current prices permitted, he was to take up exchange on France and load there with "good salts." Harris was allowed some discretion, however, in the event that "the Lord's providence shall discover any bett[r] improvement of yo[r] ketch which wee Cannot foresee." If, after advising with specified correspondents in England, a direct return seemed more feasible, the "Seaflower" was to bring back bulky goods like "course wicker flasketts, allom, Coppress, drum rims, head

---

[17] Thompson, *History of Long Island*, I, p. 438.

snares, shod shovells, window glass" etc. If a part of the freight
proceeds was to be returned, while the vessel went to France, it
was to be invested in more valuable and lighter goods, like "black
Ducape and Lutestringe." The voyage was in joint account with
other partners and the Lord was to be enlisted, not in mere form,
but as an active co-worker. "That hee may please to take the
Conduct of you, wee pray you looke carefully that hee bee wor-
shipped dayly in yor shipp, his Sabbaths Sanctifiede & all Sin
and prophainess let bee supressed."[18]

The principal products of the Colonies at that time were whale
and fish oil, whalebone, furs, deer, elk and bear skins for the
markets of Spain, Portugal, and the Straits; and refuse fish, lum-
ber, horses and provisions supplied to the West Indies. In 1690,
Massachusetts Colony made two shipments of whale oil to London, 144 barrels and 152 barrels, for account of the Treasury. A
cargo from Boston to Amsterdam included 748 barrels of oil "of
New England fishing."

Sperm whales seldom, if ever, came upon the shores of New
England. They carry in their clumsy heads spermaceti, the best
material for an illuminating candle, aside from wax, and their
blubber yields an illuminating fluid much superior to the oil of
the right whale. Sperm oil is also one of the very best lubricants
known today. The earliest mention that has been found in New
England records of a sperm whaling voyage exists in the Massachusetts Archives. In August, 1688, the commander of the brig-
antine "Happy Return," petitioned Governor Andros for "License and Permission, with one Equipage Consisting in twelve
marines, twelve whalemen and six Divers—from this Port, upon
a fishing design about the Bohames Islands, and Cap florida, for
sperma Coeti whales and Racks: and so to return to this Port."
Whether this voyage was ever undertaken we do not know.
Wrecks on the Florida coast and in the West Indies may have
proved to be a better paying proposition than whaling, but the

[18] *Hull Letter Book*, American Antiquarian Society.

petition is conclusive evidence that there were men in the Colony at that time familiar with the haunts of the sperm whale and with his capture.

The first sperm whale of which Nantucket had actual knowledge "was found dead, and ashore, on the southwest part of the island. It caused considerable excitement, some demanding a part of the prize under one pretence, some under another, and all were anxious to behold so strange an animal. There were so many claimants of the prize that it was difficult to determine to whom it should belong. The natives claimed the whale because they found it; the whites, to whom the natives made known their discovery, claimed it by a right comprehended, as they affirmed, in the purchase of the island; an officer of the Crown made his claim, and pretended to seize the fish in the name of His Majesty, as being property without any particular owner. . . . It was finally settled that the white inhabitants who first found the whale should share the prize equally amongst themselves. The teeth, considered very valuable, had been prudently taken care of by a white man and an Indian before the discovery was made public. The decision in regard to ownership certainly justified their precaution. This compromise made, the whale was cut up and the oil extracted. What the amount of it was is unknown. The sperm produced from the head was thought to be of great value for medical purposes. It was used both as an internal and an external application and such was the credulity of the people that they considered it a certain cure for all diseases; it was sought with avidity, and, for a while, was esteemed to be worth its weight in silver."[19]

The first sperm whale taken by a New England whaleman is supposed to have been captured in 1712 by Christopher Hussey of Nantucket, and the taking was the result of accident. He was cruising near the shore for right whales and was blown off shore for some distance by a strong northerly wind, where he fell in

[19] Macy, *History of Nantucket.*

with a school of sperm whales and killed one and brought its blubber home. This gave new life to the whaling business and several small vessels of about thirty tons burthen began to whale out "in the deep," as it was then called, to distinguish it from shore whaling. They fitted out for cruises of about six weeks, carried a few hogsheads, enough to contain the blubber of one whale, and after making a capture returned home to try out the oil. In 1715, Nantucket had six sloops engaged in this fishery, averaging thirty-eight tons and producing oil and bone to the value of £11000 sterling, the shore fishery, in the meantime, being still continued.[20]

The island of Nantucket is always associated with the whaling industry in New England, but its beginnings are a matter of tradition rather than recorded fact. The first Englishman to settle there was Thomas Macy who removed from Salisbury in the Massachusetts Bay in 1659. Soon after came Starbuck, Coffin and others, names famous in the history of Nantucket and of the whaling industry. Macy, the historian of the island, relates that soon after the settlement "a whale of the kind called 'scragg' came into the harbor and continued there three days. This excited the curiosity of the people and led them to devise measures to prevent its return out of the harbor. They accordingly invented and caused to be wrought for them a harpoon, with which they attacked and killed the whale. This first success encouraged them to undertake whaling as a permanent business; whales being at that time numerous in the vicinity of the shores."

In 1672, an effort was made by the islanders to induce one James Loper, who lived on the eastern end of Long Island, and afterwards at Martha's Vineyard, and carried on whaling, to come to Nantucket and "carrey on a Designe of Whale Catching," the islanders to receive one third of the profits. He was to have a monopoly of the business for two years and ten acres of land and commonage rights. John Savidge, a cooper, was also

[20] Macy, *History of Nantucket.*

granted land as an inducement to remove to the island and set up his trade, "as the Town or Whale Company have need to employ him." For some reason the project fell through for it does not appear that Loper ever lived on Nantucket. But Savidge did and doubtless shore whaling, carried on in a small way, supplied him with employment.

In 1690, further effort was made to enlarge the industry. On learning that "the people of Cape Cod had made greater proficiency in the art of whale-catching than themselves," they sent a committee to the mainland and induced Ichabod Paddock of Barnstable, to come to Nantucket and instruct them in the best method for killing whales and obtaining the oil. He proved himself an able instructor to so receptive a people, judging from the successful development of the industry in after years.

Martha's Vineyard, nearer the mainland, was settled before Nantucket and whaling began there at some time before 1652 when the town records mention the appointment of Thomas Daggett and William Weeks as "whale cutters for this year." At the town meeting held the next spring it was voted that drift whales were "to be cut out freely, four men at one time, and four at another, and so every whale, beginning at the east end of the town." Whale cutters were appointed each year thereafter and the industry flourished.

An interesting dispute arose here, in 1692, concerning a whale cast on shore which was claimed by the agents of the proprietors and also by "John Steel, harpooner, on a whale design, as being killed by him." Much debate ensued and in order to save the oil it was agreed that the agents of the proprietors should cut up the whale and try out the oil "and that no distribution be made of the said whale, or effects, till after fifteen days are expired after the date hereof, that so such persons who may pretend an interest or claim in the whale, may make their challenge; and in case such challenge appear sufficient to them, then they may deliver the said whale or oyl to the challenger; otherwise to give notice

to the proprietors, who may do as the matter may require."
James Loper, of the Vineyard, petitioned the Colonial government of Massachusetts, in 1688, for a patent for making oil and in the petition represented that he had been engaged in the whale fishery for twenty-two years.[21]

In 1692, John Higginson and Timothy Lindall, shipowners and merchants living in Salem, wrote: "We have been jointly concerned in several whale voyages to Cape Cod, and have sustained great wrong and injury by the injust dealing of the inhabitants of those parts, especially in two instances: ye first was when Woodbury and company, in our boates, in the winter of 1690, killed a large whale in Cape Cod harbour. She sank and after rose, went to sea with a harpoon, warp, etc. of ours, which have been in the hands of Nicholas Eldridge. The second case is this last winter, 1691. William Edds and company, in one of our boats, struck a whale which came ashore dead, and by ye evidence of the people of Cape Cod was the very whale they killed. The whale was taken away by Thomas Smith, of Eastham, and unjustly detained."[22] Ten years later Higginson wrote that he had "a considerable quantitie of whale oil and bone" ready for exportation and in 1706 he wrote to a friend in Ipswich of being concerned, with others, in boats for catching whales.

The whaling industry on the island of Nantucket grew rapidly in importance after 1700. The Gulf Stream makes its nearest approach to the New England coast off Nantucket and whales were plentiful without going out of sight of land. The south side of the island was divided into four equal parts and to each part was assigned a company of six men who carried on the whaling business in common. Each division covered about three and a half miles of shore line and in the middle of a division a mast was erected with a look-out at the top and near by was built a

[21] Felt, *History of Salem*, II, p. 223.
[22] Felt, *History of Salem*, II, p. 224.

hut in which the men lived. In clear weather one of the company was always in the look-out carefully scanning the sea for a sight of a spouting whale, and when seen, the boat was launched at once and the chase began.[23]

A capture made, the whale was towed ashore and the blubber stripped off in the same manner well-known at a later date. Try-works were erected on the beach and the blubber, after being sliced and minced, was "tryed out" and the oil barrelled for later shipment to Boston. After shore fishing became unprofitable these try-works still continued in use, for in the off-shore fishery, carried on in sloops and small vessels, the blubber would be cut up and stowed in hogsheads on board and brought home there to be tried out and the oil extracted. Much the same method was followed all along the New England coast where whaling was carried on. At Nantucket, Indians were largely employed in the whale fishery, each boat's crew being manned in part and sometimes wholly by Indians—and at a later date, in the palmy days of deep-sea whaling, ships usually had one or more Indians aboard—frequently expert harpooners.

The first settlers at Nantucket located themselves at the western end of the island, but as the fishery increased in importance and vessels were used it became necessary to select a better site and the location where the town now stands was determined upon and here wharves were built and new houses erected. It was the custom in winter to haul the vessels and boats on shore as a measure of protection. Boats were placed bottom upwards and lashed together and equipment was carefully stored in warehouses. Each small vessel carried two boats, one of which was held in reserve in case of accident.

The earliest recorded loss of a Nantucket whaling vessel is in 1722 when a sloop commanded by Elisha Coffin was lost at sea with all on board. Dinah, the widow of the master, in 1724 peti-

---

[23] Crevecoeur, in his *Letters of an American Farmer*, writes that when whales were sighted off Southampton, the alarm was sounded by means of a horn, when the waiting boats would be hastily manned in pursuit.

tioned the Great and General Court for legislation permitting her to marry again and in her petition she recites that "her Husband, Elisha Coffin did on the Twenty Seventh Day of April Annoq Dom: 1722 Sail from sd Island of Nantucket in a sloop: on a whaling trip intending to return in a month or six weeks at most, And Instantly a hard & dismall Storm followed; which in all probability Swallowed him and those with him up; for they were never heard of."[24]

In 1731, a sloop, commanded by Thomas Hathaway, was lost and in 1742 another sloop, Daniel Paddock, master, went down with all on board. A local historian writing in 1792, of the shore fishery, relates that "it happened once, when there were about thirty boats about six miles from the shore, that the wind came round to the northward, and blew with great violence, attended with snow. The men all rowed hard, but made but little headway. In one of the boats there were four Indians and two white men. An old Indian in the head of the boat, preceiving that the crew began to be disheartened, spake out loud in his own tongue and said, *Momadichchator auqua sarshkee Sarnkee pinchee eyoo sememoochkee chaquanks wihchee pinchee eyoo:* which in English is, Pull ahead with courage: do not be disheartened; we shall not be lost now; there are too many Englishmen to be lost now. His speaking in this manner gave the crew new courage. They soon preceived that they made headway; and after long rowing, they all got safe on shore."[25]

The importance of the Indian in the New England whale fishery had long been recognized and in 1709, by Act of Parliament for the "Encouragement of Whaling," it was provided that any Indian bound to go to sea whale fishing, between November first and April fifteenth following, should not be arrested or kept out of employment under any pretence of a contract or debt; and if any one should suffer an Indian to drink liquor during the

[24] *Mass. Archives*, IX, folio 181.
[25] *Mass. Hist. Soc. Colls.*, III, p. 157.

time when he should be at sea or at work in connection with the whale fishery, should forfeit the sum of thirty shillings. This Act was in force in 1726 and perhaps later.

The growth of the whaling industry brought about a material increase in the size and number of the vessels employed. Sloops and schooners of forty to sixty tons burthen began to cruise to the southward, remaining on that ground until July when they would return and refit and then go out for another cruise to the eastward of the Grand Bank. It soon came about that Nantucket could not furnish men enough to man the fleet and Cape Cod and Long Island were called upon to make up the deficiency. The large production of oil naturally glutted the colonial market and forced prices down, so that the Nantucket whalers began to think of a direct contact with the foreign markets.

Since the beginnings of the industry Boston merchants had acted as factors for the New England whalemen and had furnished them with needed supplies. The principal foreign market for the New England trade was London, but Amsterdam and other ports on the continent claimed a share. A mixed cargo from Boston direct to Amsterdam included 748 barrels of oil "of New England fishing."[26] As early as 1720, Nantucket made a direct shipment to the London market and the bill of lading has been preserved.[27] Its quaint phrase still possesses an interest for the descendants of old-time sailors and shipowners and those who love the sea.

> Shipped by the grace of God, in good order and well conditioned, by Paul Starbuck, in the good ship called the Hanover, whereof is master under God for the present voyage, William Chadder, and now riding in the harbour of Boston, and by God's grace bound for London; to say:—six barrels of traine oyle, being on the proper account & risque of Nathaniel Starbuck, of Nantucket, and goes consigned to Richard Part-

[26] *Mass. Archives*, LXII, folio 69.
[27] In the possession of F. C. Sanford in 1876.

ridge, Merchant in London. Being marked & numbered as in the margine & to be delivered in like good order & well conditioned at the aforesaid port of London (The dangers of the sea only excepted) unto Richard Partridge aforesaid or to his assignees, He or they paying Freight for said goods, at the rate of fifty shillings per ton, with primage & average accustomed.

In witness whereof the said Master or Purser of said Ship both affirmed to Two Bills of Lading all of this Tener and date, one of which two Bills being Accomplished, the other to stand void.

And so God send the Good Ship to her desired Port in Safety. Amen!

Articles & Contents unknown to —

[Signed]   William Chadder

Dated at Boston the 7th   4th mo.   1720

"It was found," says Macy,[28] "that Nantucket had in many places become famed for whaling, and particularly so in England, where partial supplies of oil had been received through the medium of the Boston trade. The people, finding that merchants in Boston were making a good profit by first purchasing oil at Nantucket, then ordering it to Boston, and thence shipping it to London, determined to secure the advantages of the trade to themselves, by exporting their oil in their own vessels. They had good prospects of success in this undertaking, yet, it being a new one, they moved with great caution, for they knew that a small disappointment would lead to embarrassments that would, in the end, prove distressing. They, therefore, loaded and sent out one vessel, about the year 1745. The result of this small beginning proved profitable and encouraged them to increase their shipments by sending out other vessels. They found, in addition to the profits on the sales, that the articles in return were such as their business required, viz: iron, hardware, hemp, sail cloth,

[28] Macy, *History of Nantucket*, p. 51.

and many other goods, and at a much cheaper rate than they had hitherto been subjected to."

The consumption of oil in lamps and also in the manufactures increased about this time and was a great encouragement to the whale fishery; in fact, cod and whale products were the principal exports to Great Britain from Massachusetts. But this prosperity was not long to continue. As a result of the great public expenditures in connection with the wars with the French, resulting in the conquest of Canada, Parliament looked about for new sources of revenue and in 1761 a duty was imposed on all oil and bone carried into England from the colonies. By another Act it became unlawful for a colonial vessel to find any other market and at the same time a bounty was allowed to British whalers. This unjust discrimination soon resulted in petitions to Parliament from New England merchants and London firms engaged in the colonial trade.

They represented that "in the Year 1761, The Province of the Massachusetts Bay, fitted out from Boston and other ports ten vessels of from Seventy to Ninety Tons Burden for this Purpose. That the Success of these was such as to encourage the Sending out of fifty Vessels in the Year 1762 for The same trade, That in the year 1763 more than Eighty Vessels were imploy'd in the same manner.[29] That they had already imported to London up-

[29] Out of Nantucket there's Whalemen seventy-five,
But two poor Worths among them doth survive:
There is two Ramsdills & there's Woodbury's two,
Two Ways there is, chuse which one pleaseth you,
Folgers thirteen, & Barnards there are four,
Bunkers there is three & Jenkinses no more.
Gardners there is seven, Husseys there are two,
Pinkhams there is five and a poor Delano.
Myricks there is three & Coffins there are six,
Swains there are four and one poor gally Fitch.
One Chadwick, Coggshall, Coleman there's but one,
Brown, Baxter, two & Paddacks there is three,
Wyer, Stanton, Starbuck, Moores is four you see,
But if for a Voyage I was to choose a Stanton,
I would leave Sammy out & choose Ben Stratton,
And not forget the Bocott is alive,
And that long-crotch makes up the seventy-five.
This is answering to the list, you see,
Made up in seventeen hundred & sixty-three.
                                     Whale list of Nantucket captains by
                                     Thomas Worth, 1763.

wards of 40 ton of Whale Finn; being the produce of the two first years. That upon Entring of the above Finn, a Duty was required and paid upon it, of thirty-one Pound, ten shillings per Ton. That the weight of this Duty was render'd much heavier by the great reduction made in the price of Dutch Bone since the commencement of this Trade from £ 500 to £ 300 per Ton."[30] The petition further represents that the reason for conferring the bounties on British vessels was to encourage the fishery to compete with the Dutch, yet, notwithstanding, not enough oil and bone was being brought into the English market by British vessels to supply the demand.[31] It naturally followed that the American whale fishery was soon relieved of the discriminating duty.

In 1768, Nantucket sent out eighty vessels with an average burden of seventy-five tons and probably as many more went out from other New England ports—Cape Cod, Falmouth, Dartmouth (now New Bedford), Boston, Providence, Newport, Warren and other ports engaged in the fishery to a lesser extent. These vessels sailed for Davis Straits, the Straits of Belle Isle, the Grand Banks, Gulf of St. Lawrence and the Western Islands.

The Davis Straits and northern fishery was visited by New England whalers as early as 1732, when Captain Atkins brought to Boston a Greenland bear. He went as far as 66° north. In the spring of 1737 there were a number of clearances from Boston for Davis Straits. In July, 1737, Capt. Atherton Hough took a whale "in the Straits" and two years later the August 2d issue of the Boston News-Letter states: "There is good Prospect of Success in the Whale Fishery to Greenland this Year, for several vessels are come in already, deeply laden, and others expected."

---

[30] *Massachusetts Archives*, Vol. LXVI, folio 243.

[31] Between 1759 and 1768 the Dutch sent 1324 vessels to the Greenland fishery, which captured 3,018 whales, producing 146,419 barrels of oil and 8,785,140 pounds of bone. Great Britain during the same period sent out about one-third the number of vessels. Scoresby, *Account of the Arctic Regions and the Northern Whale Fishery*, Edinburgh, 1820.

The *New England Journal* of April 19, 1737, says of Province-town, Mass.: "There are now fitting out from this Place a dozen sail of vessels (and some of them burthen'd a Hundred Tons) bound for Davis Straights on the Whaling Design and are just ready to sail. So many of our People are now bound on this Voyage, that there will not be left behind above a Dozen or Four-teen men in the Town."

In 1748, Parliament passed an Act to encourage this fishery which had languished because of the war with France. A bounty of twenty shillings a ton was granted to ships engaged in whaling during the existing war and harpooners and whalemen engaged in the Greenland fishery were exempted from impressment. All whalers must remain in the Davis Straits from May until August 20th unless sooner full of oil or obliged to return by accident.

In 1761, after the conquest of Canada, the New England whalemen reaped a rich harvest in the Gulf of St. Lawrence and the Straits of Belle Isle.

The *Boston News-Letter* for Aug. 8, 1765, has the following:
"Tuesday one of the sloops which has been on the Whaling Business returned here. We hear that the Vessels employed in the Whale Fishery from this and the neighbouring Maritime Towns, amounting to near 100 sail, have been very successful this Season in the Gulph of St. Lawrence and Streights of Belle Isle; having tis said, already made upwards of 9,000 Barrels of Oil." Two weeks later the *News-Letter* reported that news had been received from the whaling fleet on the Labrador coast and that the vessels were in difficulties in consequence of orders is-sued by the captain of His Majesty's sloop "Zephyr," stationed on that coast, who had decreed that refuse parts of whales must be left at least three leagues from the shore to prevent damage to the cod and seal fishery; that no trade or intercourse might be carried on with the French; that the Indians must be treated with the greatest civility and on no account were they to be sup-plied with spirituous liquors; that no passengers could be trans-

ported to the Plantations and no other fishing might be carried
on than whaling.

It was this last regulation that fell most heavily on the New
England whalemen who were accustomed to go north prepared
for either the cod or the whale fishing. If whales were scarce then
the cod lines were used. It is not surprising that the *News-Letter* records that "Since our last, several Vessels are returned from
the Whaling Business, who have not only had very bad Success,
but also have been ill-treated by some of the Cruisers on the La-
bradore Coast." This regulation controlling the cod fishery was
inforced under a pretense that the coast had been patented to a
Company by the Governor of Newfoundland and Labrador.

In consequence of these orders and the strict supervision of
the King's ships on the Labrador Station, many of the whaling
fleet left the coast and went to the banks. The year 1766 proved
to be a poor season for the northern whale fishery. Under date
of Oct. 2, 1766, the *Boston News-Letter* says: "Since our last
a Number of Vessels have arrived from Whaling. They have not
been successful generally. One of them, viz: Capt. Clark, on
Thursday Morning last discovered a Spermaceti Whale near
George's Banks, mann'd his Boat and gave Chase to her, and
she coming up with her jaws against the Bow of the Boat struck
it with such violence that it threw a Son of the Captain; (who
was forward ready with his Lance) a considerable Height from
the Boat, and when he fell the Whale turned with her devouring
Jaws opened, and caught him. He was heard to scream, when
she closed her Jaws, and part of his Body was seen out of her
mouth, when she turned and went off."

One of the results of the restrictions enforced on the Straits
of Belle Isle whaling ground was the sending out of whaling ven-
tures to the Western Islands, the Cape de Verdes and the banks
off the Brazilian coast. Nearly fifty New England whalers went
to these southern latitudes during the year 1767. Whales at that

time were also pursued along the edge of the Gulf Stream and there they continued to be found for many years.

The following year found many whalers again on the Labrador coast as a result of a report, current in New England, that the irksome regulations had been revoked. The last of April, 1768, saw about sixty whalers anchored in Man-of-War Cove, Canso Gut, surrounded with drift ice. On May 23d they were still there and that day cleared their decks of snow which was "almost over shoes deep."

In addition to the normal dangers of the whale fishery, there were times when the whalemen were in danger of capture by privateers and even pirates. The French and Spanish privateers were on the New England coast in 1741 and in May a whaling vessel out of Barnstable, commanded by Capt. Solomon Sturgis, was captured. The captain and eight hands were dismissed, but John Davis, the mate, and four men were carried off in the sloop. The frequency of privateers seems to have prevented the sending out of whalers to the Davis Straits, for the Boston newspapers report no departures or arrivals from that ground for several years.

A French privateer made several captures in 1744 near Nantucket and in Vineyard Sound and landed many of her prisoners on the Island. During the years 1755 and 1756, six Nantucket whalers were lost at sea and six were taken by the French and destroyed, the crews being carried away into captivity. In 1768, eighty whalers sailed from Nantucket but only seventy returned. The missing ten were either captured by the French or lost at sea and this ratio of disaster seems to have prevailed elsewhere.

The *Boston News-Letter* preserves an account of an adventure that happened to two Nantucket whaling sloops while lying at anchor in the harbor of Abaco, one of the Bahama Islands. A ship appeared off the mouth of the harbor with her signals set asking for assistance. One of the whaling captains at once made up a boat's crew and rowed out to the ship. On reaching the vessel's side and boarding her, he was surprised to have a pistol presented to his head by the officer in command with a demand that he should pilot the ship into the harbor. Nothing else was to be done and soon the ship was at anchor where a point of land lay between her and the sloops. This done, the boat was dismissed and the men returned to their vessels. The Nantucket captains now held a consultation as to what course should be pursued. As those who had been on board the stranger noticed that the men seemed to be armed and that a man was alone in the cabin, it was concluded that the ship was in the hands of pirates and that the man in the cabin was the former captain.

Measures were immediately taken to secure the vessel and crew. An invitation was extended to the usurping captain, his officers and passengers, to dine on board one of the sloops and this was accepted. At the appointed time the supposed pirate captain, his boatswain and the man seen in the cabin, as representative of the passengers, came on board the sloop. As the dinner progressed the supposed pirate became uneasy and proposed to return to his vessel, whereupon he was at once seized by the whalemen and bound. The passenger, who was in fact the actual captain, as had been supposed, then related what had happened.

The ship had sailed from Bristol, R. I., bound for the coast of Africa on a slaving voyage. The slaves had been landed in the West Indies and a return cargo of sugar had been taken aboard, and not long after this a mutiny occurred, the mutineers intending to become pirates, a business at that time quite thrifty and promising.

The whalemen now told the boatswain, who had come aboard with the pirate captain, if he would go on board the ship and return with the former mate, who was in irons, and also aid in recapturing the vessel, they would use their best endeavors to have him cleared from the penalties of the law. They also prudently intimated to him that there was a man-of-war within two hours sail from which they could obtain assistance, and he was told that they would set a certain signal when they had secured help from the ship of war.

The boatswain not returning according to agreement, one of the sloops weighed anchor and stood toward the pirate as though to pass on one side of her. As she approached, the mutineers shifted their guns over to the side on which it seemed apparent she would pass and trained them so as to sink her as she sailed by. But the whalemen on the sloop were alive to their intentions and as she neared the ship her course was suddenly changed and she swept by on the other side and was out of range of the guns before the pirates could reshift and train their cannon.

The sloop continued on her course until she was out of sight of the ship. She then tacked, set the signal agreed with the boatswain that help had been secured from the man-of-war, and returning steered boldly for the ship. As she hove in sight, the pirates, recognizing the signal and believing an armed force from the man-of-war was on board, abandoned the ship and made for the shore in their boats where, not long after, they were run down and taken into custody. The whalemen boarded their prize, released the mate, and brought the ship into New Providence where a bounty of $2500. was allowed them. As for the would-be pirate captain—he was hanged.

Whalemen were in danger of capture by pirates not only to the southward, near the West Indies, but also in home waters, almost within sight of their own anchorages. Early in the eighteenth century piracy was common everywhere, and with the coming of spring the pirate captains, who had remained in the warm waters of the West Indies during the winter months, would cruise northward along the coast capturing small vessels in the hope of obtaining provisions and also looting larger craft bound to and from Europe or the Leeward Islands.

Between 1722 and 1724, one of the most dreaded of these pirates was Capt. Ned Low, a bloodthirsty scoundrel who had lived in Boston for some years, where he married a respectable girl and had children. He was a rigger by trade and having been discharged by his employer shipped on a sloop bound for the Bay of Honduras for a cargo of logwood. While there he became a pirate and meeting with success he soon became captain of a sloop and later commanded a well-manned ship. Within twenty months he took one hundred and forty vessels.

On June 10th, 1723, Low, in the sloop "Fortune," was off the eastern end of Long Island with his consort, the sloop "Ranger," when the man-of-war "Greyhound," of 20 guns and 120 men, on the New York Station, came in sight and after a two hours' fight captured the "Ranger" and took thirty-seven whites and six negroes into Newport, where the captain and twenty-five of his men were hanged on gallows set up between high and low water mark.

When Low saw that his consort could not escape, he showed the real stuff that he was made of and bore away leaving the "Ranger" to her fate. But his rage and chagrin knew no bounds and swearing many oaths he vowed vengeance on the unfortunates that next fell into his hands. This happened only two days later when he came upon a sloop out of Nantucket that was whale fishing about eighty miles off shore. She had two whale-boats and one of them fortunately was out and at some considerable distance from the sloop at the time she was taken. The men in this boat, seeing what had happened, got safely to another whaling sloop some distance away and all escaped.

The captain of the captured sloop was Nathan Skiff, a young unmarried man living on Nantucket. Low first ordered him stripped and then cruelly whipped him about the deck. His ears were then slashed off. After a time they grew tired of beating the unfortunate man and telling him that because he had been a good captain he should have an easy death, at last they shot him through the head and sunk the sloop. Low "forced" a boy and two Indians and allowed three others of the crew to go away in a whaleboat in which, fortunately, there was a little water and a few biscuits, and with good weather these men at last reached Nantucket safely—"beyond all expectation," ends the account in the *Boston News-Letter*.

Low's insane rage was unabated two days later when a fishing boat was taken off Block Island. The master was dragged on board the pirate sloop and Low with furious oaths at once attacked the unfortunate man with a cutlass and hacked off his head. He gave the boat to two Indians who sailed with the murdered man and sent them away with the information that he intended to kill the master of every New England vessel he captured. On the afternoon of the same day two whaling sloops out of Plymouth were taken near the Rhode Island shore. The master of one vessel he ripped open alive and taking out the poor man's heart ordered it roasted and then compelled the mate to eat it. The master of the other sloop he slashed and mauled about the deck and then cut off his ears and had them roasted and after sprinkling with salt and pepper, made the unfortunate man eat them. His wounds were so severe that he afterwards died.[32] Low proposed to murder some of the hands on these whaling sloops but the pirate crew had had enough blood about the deck for one day and swore the rest of the men should go free so Low was obliged to submit. These men brought home the information that the pirate master and crew claimed to have on board nearly £150,000 value in gold and silver coin and plate.[33]

By the middle of the eighteenth century the increased use of lamps made whale oil a necessity. In 1742 it sold in the English market at £18.0.13 per tun and ten years later it was bringing £21. In 1770, the American colonies were exporting 5667 tuns of whale oil, most of it going to England, valued at £83.012, while the production of bone that year amounted to 112,971 pounds valued at £19.121.

[32] *Boston News-Letter*, June 27, 1723.
[33] *The Pirates of the New England Coast*, Salem, 1923, page 210.

John Adams, in his "Diary," records the substance of a conversation with William Pitt, in which he remarked to the English statesman that "the fat of the spermaceti-whale gives the clearest and most beautiful flame of any substance that is known in nature, and we are surprised that you prefer darkness, and consequent robberies, burglaries, and murders in your streets, to the receiving, as a remittance, our spermaceti oil. The lamps around Grosvenor Square, I knew, and in Downing Street, too, I supposed, are dim by midnight, and extinguished by two o'clock; whereas our oil would burn bright till 9 o'clock in the morning."[34]

The town of Boston in New England supplied itself with street lights on March 2, 1773, when nearly three hundred lamps were lighted for the first time. "They will be of great utility to this metropolis," remarked the editor of the *Massachusetts Gazette*. At a much earlier date, however, public spirited persons in Boston had set lamps outside their houses, to light the narrow streets.

In the early days many New England families made dipped candles, and a better grade was cast in moulds. Tallow candles were also manufactured in many of the larger towns and became an article of commerce early in the eighteenth century. In November, 1700, the town of Boston granted liberty to Capt. Nathaniel Byfield, Capt. Andrew Belcher and others, "to set up a furnace or kiddle for melting tallow in order to make candles."

The manufacture of candles from sperm oil was projected in New England as early as 1749 when Benjamin Crabb of the town of Rehoboth petitioned the Massachusetts General Court for "the Sole priviledge of making Candles of Coarse Sperma Caeti Oyle." He represented that he had been at great expense in providing himself with proper implements and if duly encouraged he proposed to undertake the manufacture of sperm candles and to instruct others in the art. The Representatives enacted a bill

[34] *Works of John Adams*, VIII, pp. 308-309.

granting Crabb and his heirs sole rights for a term of fourteen years, which the Council amended by reducing the period to ten years, and requiring that Crabb should set up his works within seven miles of Boston. There was also a provision providing for enactment in case "no other Person in the Province has the Art of pressing, fluxing and chrystalizing of Sperma Ceti and course Sperma Ceti Oyle, and of making Candles of the same."[35]

Crabb did not accept the provisions of the special legislation enacted for his benefit and Macy in his "History of Nantucket" states that he removed to Rhode Island where he set up a works that was destroyed by fire within a short time. In 1753, Obadiah Brown erected a candle-works near Providence and Crabb was placed in charge of the manufactory. Crabb proved to be less capable than Brown supposed and the secret of refining was at last acquired by Brown as a result of his own experiments. Moses Lopez, a Jewish merchant at Newport, engaged in the same business in 1755 and was soon followed by others.

In 1746 there arrived in Boston two young men from Devon, England—Joseph Palmer and Richard Cranch—who opened a wool-card manufactory, which was so successful that six years later they acquired a large tract of land in Braintree, in that part of Quincy known as Germantown, and built a chocolate mill and spermaceti and glass works. Josiah Quincy was also concerned in the spermaceti works and petitioned the General Court, Dec. 12, 1752, for the privilege of carrying on the candle manufactory under a new process stating that "a person lately from England, well skilled in the Art of Refining Sperma Caetia from the Oyle, and making the same into Candals, has applied to him for employment in the business, that he has invented a new Machine for the more easy expressing the Oyl from the Sperma as also sundry Utensils never before used to the great improvement of the manufacture."

The person "lately from England" was one John Surah, and

[35] *Massachusetts Archives*, Vol. LIX, folio 369.

[2] ENGRAVED SHEET USED BY JOSEPH PALMER & CO., OF BOSTON, AS
EARLY AS 1754, TO ADVERTISE THEIR MANUFACTURE
OF SPERMACETI CANDLES.

From an engraving by Nathaniel Hurd.

less than four months later he, too, petitioned the General Court, representing the "sundry Hardships he has suffered by the unjust Treatment of Mr Josiah Quincy, of Braintree, and as he is a Stranger in the Country, he prays the Intoposition and Protection of the Country."[36] It is quite evident that the two men had fallen out over the project for making "Candals" from "Sperma Caetia."

The manufacture continued, however, and turned out to be a business success. In November, 1761, the eight manufacturers of spermaceti candles located in New England, at the suggestion of Richard Cranch & Co., of Braintree, entered into an association under the name of "The United Company of Spermaceti Candlers," in order to control the manufacture. The agreement was to be in force for seventeen months.[37] Orders were to be sent to buyers of head matter not to pay more than £6 per tun above the price of sperm body brown oil and the price for the latter was to be determined by the current price given by Boston merchants for the London market on the day the purchaser received the head matter. Agents buying the same were not to receive above 2½ per cent commission. Spermaceti candles were not to be sold within the limits of New England at less than one shilling, ten pence, half penny per pound, with an extra charge of a shilling for each box, to contain about a quarter of a hundred weight. None of the parties to the agreement was allowed to take on any new partners without the consent of the other firms. In case it should come about that the price for head matter should remain above £6 per tun more than the price for oil, the association agreed to fit out at least twelve vessels to be employed in the whale fishery on joint account. They also agreed to use "all fair and honourable means to prevent the setting up by any other Spermaceti works."

Those who engaged in this trust were Obadiah Browne & Co.,

---

[36] *Massachusetts House Journal.*
[37] It was renewed from time to time and lasted for a number of years.

Providence, R. I.; Richard Cranch & Co. and Edward Langdon & Co., Boston; Napthali Hart & Co., Isaac Stelle & Co., Thomas Robinson & Co., Aaron Lopez & Co., and Collins & Rivera, all of Newport. There also was a firm in Philadelphia whose name does not appear. Seven factors of the association were located at Nantucket, one at Newport, one at Providence and one at Boston.[38] The process of manufacture was so carefully kept a secret that it was not until 1772 that the people of Nantucket were able to carry on the business there. The first candle house in New Bedford was built about the same time.

As the years passed and the time drew near when the Colonies should test their strength with the Mother Country, the whaling business increased to an extent unimagined. In 1775 there were over three hundred and fifty New England vessels engaged in the whale fishery, some of them of large tonnage for the times. Other trades were interested in the success of the whalers — the rope-maker, the cooper, the blacksmith, the carpenter and those who worked at shipbuilding. While a ship was at sea the owners at home were occupied in procuring supplies and equipment needed for the next voyage and so a considerable number of persons became interested directly or indirectly in the success of the fishery.

"The cooper, while employed in making the casks, took care that they were of sound and seasoned wood, lest they might leak his oil in the long voyage; the blacksmith forged his choicest iron in the shank of the harpoon, which he knew, perhaps from actual knowledge, would be put to the severest test in wrenching and twisting, as the whale, in which he had a one-hundredth interest, was secured; the rope-maker faithfully tested each yarn of the tow-line, to make certain that it would carry two hundred pounds' strain, for he knew that one weak inch in his work might lose to him his share in a fighting monster."[39]

---

[38] *Commerce of Rhode Island*, Vol. I, pp. 80-92; 97-100.
[39] Davis, *Nimrod of the Sea*, pp. 48, 49.

Whaling was carried on at that time in Nantucket, Wellfleet, Dartmouth (New Bedford), Martha's Vineyard, Barnstable, Falmouth, Swansey and Boston, in Massachusetts; in Newport, Providence, Warren and Tiverton, in Rhode Island; in New London, Conn., and Sag Harbor on Long Island; and in all of these ports there was employment and to spare for any one concerned in the fishery. Then came the Revolution and with it the destruction of the industry, save on the island of Nantucket, where a desperate struggle for existence kept vessels at sea. The war over, with thousands of whalemen released from service on land and sea, the fishery soon regained its importance among the industries of the nation—a story that has been told and retold and never lost its savor.

WHALE SHIPS AND WHALING
A PICTORIAL HISTORY OF WHALING
DURING THREE CENTURIES

L I B E R   X X.

De glacialibus Inſtrumentis.

[3] INSTRUMENTS USED IN THE ICE BY 16TH CENTURY WHALERS.

D E   P I S C I B.   M O N S T R O.

De ſuffocatione nauium per monſtroſos Piſces.

[4] A WHALE SWALLOWING A SHIP.

From wood engravings in "Historia de Gentibus Septentrionalibus," 1555, in the Macpherson Collection.

De pugna Balenæ contra Orcam.

[5] FIGHT BETWEEN A WHALE AND A THRASHER.

LIBER XXI.

De modo piscandi Cetos, & Balenas.

[6] CUTTING UP A WHALE.

From wood engravings in "Historia de Gentibus Septentrionalibus,"
1555, in the Macpherson Collection.

De fpermate Ceti, quod Ambra dicitur,
& eius Medicinis.

[7] SPERM WHALE FISHING.

DE PISCIB. MONSTRO.

De Pifcibus Islandiæ.

[8] ICELAND FISHERY AT OSTRABORD.

From wood engravings in "Historia de Gentibus Septentrionalibus,"
1555, in the Macpherson Collection.

[9] WHALING SCENE NEAR NOVA ZEMBLA IN 1596.
From an etching by Jan Luyken in the Macpherson Collection.

[10] A DUTCH SHIP IN THE ICE NEAR SPITZBERGEN, AUG. 26, 1596.
From an engraving in "Barentz' Voyages," Venice, 1699, in the Macpherson Collection.

[11] DUTCH SHIP IN THE ICE NEAR SPITZBERGEN, AUG. 27, 1596.
From an engraving in "Barentz' Voyages," in the Macpherson Collection.

[12] DUTCH WHALEMEN ATTACKED BY BEARS AS THEY WERE
REMOVING STORES FROM THEIR ABANDONED SHIP.

From an engraving in "Barentz' Voyages," in the Macpherson Collection.

[13] THE DEPARTURE OF THE BOATS, JULY, 1597, NEAR SPITZ-
BERGEN.
From an engraving in "Barentz' Voyages," in the Macpherson Collection.

XLII.

NAVI NOSTRA GLACIEI
CVMVLIS DEFIXA, NOSTRVM
tres prope merfi. 7.

Oftquam glaciei obiectu perpetuo noftrum curfum præ-pediri intelleximus, vnanimi confenfu retrò in Hollandiam reuerti ftatuentes, iam primùm circumquaque congelato mari nos obfeptos animaduertimus, ita vt nec porro, nec retrò curfus nobis patefceret. N̄ autarum er-go tribus ad refcindendam glaciem, adeoque nobis eru-ptum parandum è naui demiffis, accidit, vt glacie fua fponte diruta & foluta, illi periclitarentur haud leuiter. Qui tamen mutuo cæterorum au-xilio nauis retinaculis acceptis, ita erepti & feruati funt.

[14] BARENTZ SHIP IN THE ICE NEAR SPITZBERGEN, AUG. 26, 1596.
From the engraving by De Bry, 1601, in the Macpherson Collection.

XL VII.
EXPRESSA DOMVS NOSTRAE
HYBERNÆ FORMA SEV SPECIES. 12.

Omus extructa hæc fere figura erat. In medio focus erat, supra quem caminus ex asseribus extructus tectum excedebat. Ad latera suffixa scamna erant, ita separata & interstincta, vt discretus cuilibet locus ad lectum ponendum daretur. Parte vna dolium quoddam grandius stabat, quod nobis pro balneo faciebat, aut sudario. Ad huius angulum proximum automatum appendebat: quod tamen immensi frigoris vi tandem immotum factum est. Ideoq, in eius locum horologium arenarium sufficere coacti sumus, quod singulis horis 12. inaniebatur. Superne è mediæ domus tabulato lampas propendebat noctes atq, dies lucida: ad cuius lumen temporis tædium, canendo, legendoq, & exercitijs alijs fallebamus.

[15] HOUSE IN WHICH BARENTZ SPENT THE WINTER OF 1596-1597, IN SPITZBERGEN.

From the engraving by De Bry, 1601, in the Macpherson Collection.

I.
DE INDORVM MIRA PISCA-
TIONIS RATIONE.

ISCATVI *operam daturi Indi, hunc ferè modum tenent. Balenis grandioribus insi-*
dias structuri, scaphis exiguis in mare remigant quolibet sua priuata scapha recepto.
Cetum ergò si alicubi quempiam in conspectum se offerentem Indus notant, scapha ad
eum properant, in eius dorsum exilit, palosq̃, binos in hunc vsum paratos, ligneos, eius
in nares vel potius aures ex quibus piscis conceptas aquas subinde eructat, demittit.
Et quamuis interim piscis sese nunc submittat, nunc eleuet, nihilo tamen ignauior pisca-
tor, dorso obstinatè insistit, dum penitus palos in profundos istos meatus demerserit. Quo
facto, rursus in scapham prosilit, & sune, quem palo abscissurus adalligauit, iugi tractu
piscem allicit, dum tandem eum propter aeris, naribus hauriendi defectum lassatum & infirmatum in littus
seu aridum extrahat. Quem tandem illic in partes dirimunt, & inter socios aqua ratione dispensant.   Sed
& piscatus sui modum alium exercent, retibus iactatis faciliorem. Iuncos magna copia ex ordine colligant. Il-
lis non secus ac equites equis insidentes, incitatis ligneis remis, quò lubet, pergunt.   Locum despicati idoneum
sua retia iactant, dum, quantum piscium capturierunt, caperunt. Iis asseruatis, ad terram redeunt, nauiculám-
que vndis extractam, vt resiccetur, expandunt aut extendunt. Sicut in historia contextu ista fusius percen-
sentur.

[16] NATIVES HUNTING WHALES OFF MADAGASCAR IN 1598.
From the engraving by De Bry, 1601, in the Macpherson Collection.

IV.
QVA INDVSTRIA BARBARI
IN S. MARIÆ INSVLA CETOS
capiant.

*ᴺᴰᴵ S. Mariæ insulæ accola, cetos hoc ferè modo captant.
Vbi morentur, prius attendunt. Ad proditum vnum scaphis suis applicant : & vnius lapidis iactu absistentes, ha-
mum seu vncum ferreum, oblongo ex arborum corticibus
fune religatum, in corpus eius eiaculantur. Altera ergò funis extremita-
te in scaphis retenta, piscem tamdiu attrabunt, dum & penitus longo ex-
ercitio ille fatigetur, & renisu valentiore vulnus augeatur grandescatq̃,
isque adeò cruoris copiosioris emanatione infirmetur & q. emoriatur.
Hoc impetrato, in vadum eum extrabunt : extractum laniant : & suam
quilibet portionem auferunt.*

b

[17] NATIVES HUNTING WHALES.
From an engraving by De Bry, 1602, in the Macpherson Collection.

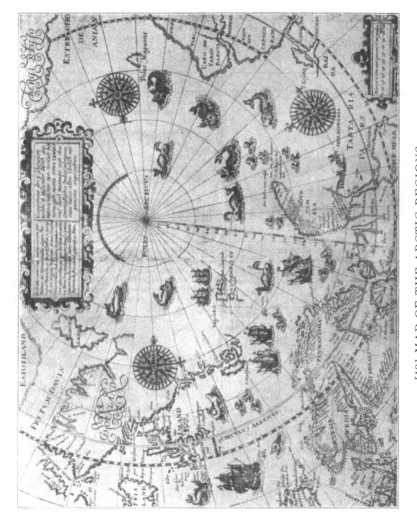

[18] MAP OF THE ARCTIC REGIONS.

From the engraving by De Bry, 1601, in the Macpherson Collection.

A Whale is ordinarly about 60 foote longe

The whale is cut up as hee lyes floting crofse the ftearne of a shipp the blubber is cut from the flesh by peeces 3 or 4 foote long and being rafed is rowed on fhore towards the coppers

When the whale comes aboue water ȳ shallop rowes towards him and being within reach of him the harpoiner darts his harpingiron at him out of both his hands and being faft they lance him to death

They place 2. or 3. coppers on a rve and ȳ chopping boat on the one fide and the cooling boate on the other fide to receiue ȳ oyle of ȳ coppers, the chopt blubber being boyled is taken out of the coppers and put in wiker bafkets or barowes throwȳ wᵗʰ the oyle is dreaned and rünes into ȳ cooler wᶜʰ us ½ fallᵒ water out of wᶜʰ it is conuaied by troughs into buts or hogsheads

[19] WHALING AT SPITZBERGEN IN 1611.   PLATE I.
From engravings in Hans Egede's "Beschryving van Oud-Groenland," re-engraved for "Churchill's Voyages," London, 1745, Vol. IV, page 743.

Panel text (top left): When the whale is killed hee is in this mann[er] towed to the shipps by twoe or three shal: lops made fast one to another.

Panel text (top right): Thus they make cleane and scrape y͏e whale fins

Panel text (bottom left): The peeces of blubber are towed to the shore side by a shallop and drawne onshore by a crane or caried by twoe menn on a [ ] barrowe to y͏e twoe cutters w[ch] cutts them the [ ] breadt of a tr[ ]encher and [ ] very thine & [ ] by twoe boys [ ] are caried [ ] w handhooks [ ] to y͏e choppers

Panel text (bottom right): A tent and Coopers at worke

[20] WHALING AT SPITZBERGEN IN 1611.   PLATE II.

From engravings in Hans Egede's "Beschryving van Oud-Groenland," re-engraved for "Churchill's Voyages," Vol. IV, page 743.

[21] THE CELEBRATION OF MASS ON THE BACK OF A WHALE.

From an engraving in "Nova Typis Transacta Navigato," Manacho, 1621, in the Frank Wood Collection.

[22] MAP OF NOVA ZEMBLA IN 1630.
From "God's Power and Providence," by Edward Pelham, London, 1631.

[23] WHALE FISHING AND KILLING MORSSES.
From an engraving in Marten's "Voyage into Spitzbergen and Greenland,"
London, 1711.

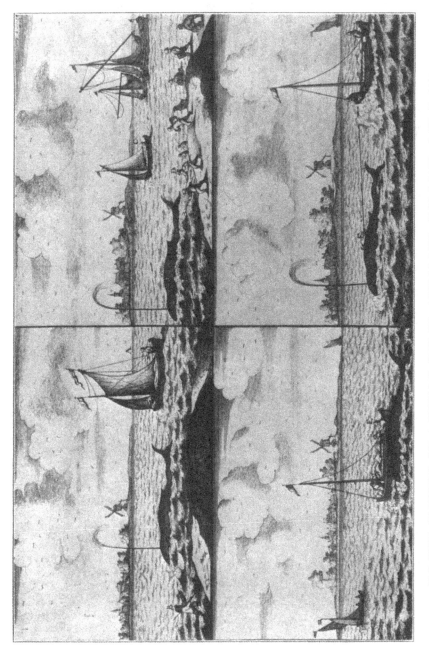

[24] THE CAPTURE OF A WHALE OFF ST. ANNALAND, HOLLAND, OCT. 7, 1682.
From a Dutch engraving in the Macpherson Collection.

[25] A DUTCH WHALER IN THE NOVA ZEMBLA FISHERY.

From an engraving by C. Moy in J. A. van Oelen's work on whaling, Leyden, 1684.

[26] QUI SICCIS OCULIS MONSTRA NATANTIA QUI VIDIT MARE TURGIDUM.

The Greenland Whale Fishery — an engraving after a drawing by A. Vander Laan, 1700, in the Macpherson Collection.

[27] THE GREENLAND WHALE FISHERY.

From a mezzotint by T. Willson after a drawing by Vdr. Maulen, published in London about 1700, in the Macpherson Collection.

[64]

[28] WHALING IN THE GREENLAND FISHERY.

From an engraving by E. Kirkhall, after T. Baston, in the Allan Forbes Collection.

[29] A REPRESENTATION OF THE FISHERY OF GREAT BRITAIN.
From an engraving by E. Kirkhall (*ca.* 1720) after T. Baston, in the Macpherson
Collection.

[30] GREENLAND AND THE WHALE FISHERY. SHIPS SAILING THROUGH THE ICE IN SEARCH AFTER WHALES.

From an engraving published about 1740 by Carington Bowles, in the Macpherson Collection.

The Long boats making towards a WHALE & the Harponiers going to cast their Lances at him.

Paued for Carington Bowles, Map & Printseller N° 69 in St Pauls Church Yard, London

[31] From a colored engraving in the Macpherson Collection.

A WHALE swimming with great Force & Celerity after the Harpoons from its feet in him.

[32] From a colored engraving in the Macpherson Collection.

[33] From a colored engraving in the Macpherson Collection.

the WHALE diving to the bottom after he is struck with the Harpoon Iron; & the Harpooners standing
in readiness to extend Irons at fresh with Spears; when he rises again

[34] From a colored engraving in the Macpherson Collection.

[35] From a colored engraving in the Macpherson Collection.

The Sailors attacking the White BEAR with their Spears, which are frequently flinging upon the Ice in the North Seas.
Printed for Carrington Bowles Map & Printseller N° 69 in St Pauls Church Yard London.

[36] From a colored engraving in the Macpherson Collection.

[73]

The Flinging of the WHALE, in order to Cut it up to Freight the Ship –

[37] From a colored engraving in the Macpherson Collection.

The Indians shooting the REIN DEER, which are frequently on the Rocks of Ice.—
Printed for Carington Bowles Map & Printseller N.º69 in S.¹ Pauls Church Yard, London.—

[38] From a colored engraving in the Macpherson Collection.

The manner of killing & knocking on the head the SEA LION, on the Ice; has Tusks which are about 2 Foot long are whiter & more valuable than Ivory

Painted for Cavington, Newbery Map & Printseller No 82 in S Pauls Church Yard, London.

[39] From a colored engraving in the Macpherson Collection.

[76]

A SHIP driven by Storm, and wrecked amongst the Ice and Isles

[40] From a colored engraving in the Macpherson Collection.

[77]

Ships Freighted with Whale; | lading out of the Ice for Home?
Printed for Carrington Bowles May 9 1784 as 3 pards Church yard London'. –

[41] From a colored engraving in the Macpherson Collection.

[42] THE WHALE FISHERY IN THE ARCTIC REGIONS.

French colored engraving in the Macpherson Collection, after an English engraving, *ca.* 1740.

La grande Pêche des Baleines figurée au naturel et telle que les Hollandois, les Hambourgeois et autres Nations la font tous les ans dans le Détroit de Davis, sur les Côtes de Groenland.

[43] DUTCH AND HAMBURG WHALERS FISHING IN DAVIS STRAITS OFF THE COAST OF GREENLAND. From a French engraving, published in 1754, in the Macpherson Collection.

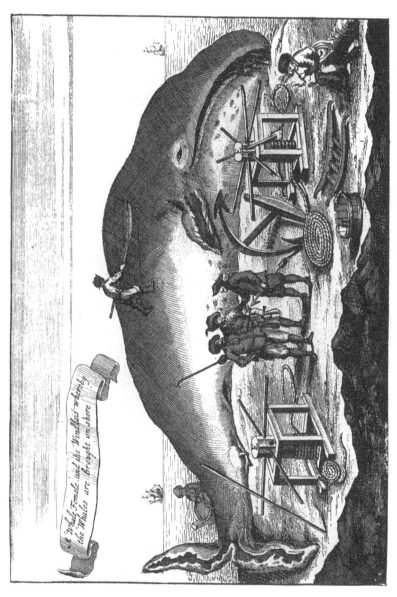

A Whale Female and the Windlass whereby the Whales are brought on shore

[44] From an engraving in Monck's "Account of a most dangerous Voyage to Greenland," in "Churchill's Voyages," Vol. I. London, 1744.

[45] THE MANNER OF CATCHING WHALES.

From an engraving in Monck's "Account of a most dangerous Voyage to Greenland," in "Churchill's Voyages," Vol. I, London, 1744.

[46] THE GREENLAND FISHERY.

From an engraving published by J. Boydell, London, 1754, in the Macpherson Collection.

[47] A VIEW OF THE WHALE FISHERY.

Colored engraving from the "Universal Magazine," London, 1760, in the Macpherson Collection.

[48] THEY STAND READY TO STICK THE WHALE.
From an engraving by A. Vander Laan, *ca.* 1780, in the Macpherson Collection.

De Walvis heurd en voeld de wyl men is aan 't | Der Wallfisch wendet sich und wühlet in dessen man ihn
Lensen. | mit einem Spies sticht, oder die seiten durch bohret.
The whale is troubled and turns her self whilst people are sticking her.

[49] THE WHALE IS TROUBLED AND TURNS HERSELF.
From an engraving by A. Vander Laan, *ca.* 1780, in the Macpherson Collection.

De Walvis wort na Boord gehoogeert of gerved. | Der Wallfisch wird ans Schiff gerudert.
The whale is brought or Rowed to the Ship.

[50] THE WHALE IS BROUGHT TO THE SHIP.
From an engraving by A. Vander Laan, *ca.* 1780, in the Macpherson Collection.

[51] THEY CUT THE WHALE IN PIECES.
From an engraving by A. Vander Laan, *ca.* 1780, in the Allan Forbes Collection.

The Boiling the fat out of the whale.

[52] THE BOILING THE FAT OUT OF THE WHALE.
From an engraving by A. Vander Laan, *ca.* 1780, in the Allan Forbes Collection.

View of the WHALE FISHERY, &c. in Greenland.

[53] From an engraving made in 1781, in the Macpherson Collection.

[54] THE NORTHERN WHALE FISHERY.
From an engraving by M. Sallieth (1782), after a drawing by H. Kobell, Jr. (1778), in the Allan Forbes Collection.

[55] A VIEW OF THE WHALE FISHERY ON THE COAST OF GREENLAND
From an engraving by Thornton, *ca.* 1782, in the Macpherson Collection.

[56] A DUTCH WHALER BOUND ON A GREENLAND VOYAGE.
From an engraving in Groenewegen, *Hollandse Scheepen*, Amsterdam, 1789, in
the Clark Collection, Massachusetts Institute of Technology.

[57] A DUTCH WHALER OFF THE COAST OF GREENLAND.
From an engraving in Groenewegen, *Hollandse Scheepen*, Amsterdam, 1789, in
the Clark Collection, Massachusetts Institute of Technology.

[58] THE GREENLAND WHALE FISHERY.

From an aquatint by Dodd, published in 1789 by Boydell, London, in the Macpherson Collection.

[59] THE NORTH WEST OR DAVIS STRAITS WHALE FISHERY.
From an aquatint by R. Dodd, published by Boydell, London, 1789, in the Macpherson Collection.

[60] THE GREENLAND WHALE FISHERY.
From an engraving by Wallis, 1805, after Craig, in the Macpherson
Collection.

[61] VIEW OF PETERHEAD, SCOTLAND, SHOWING WHALERS IN THE HARBOR.
From an aquatint, after a painting by George Tytler, 1813, in the Clark Collection, Massachusetts Institute of Technology.

[62] BOATS APPROACHING A WHALE.

Colored aquatint by Dubourg, after J. H. Clark, London, 1813, in the Macpherson Collection.

[63] SHOOTING THE HARPOON AT A WHALE.

From a colored aquatint by Dubourg, after J. H. Clark, London, 1813, in the Macpherson Collection.

[64] A SHIP'S BOAT ATTACKING A WHALE.

Colored aquatint by Dubourg, after J. H. Clark, London, 1813, in the Macpherson Collection.

[65] A WHALE BROUGHT ALONG-SIDE A SHIP.

Colored aquatint by Dubourg, after J. H. Clark, London, 1813, in the Macpherson Collection.

[66] DANGERS OF THE WHALE FISHERY.
From an engraving in Scoresby's "Account of the Arctic Regions,"
Edinburgh, 1820.

[67] A WHALE UPSETTING A BOAT.

From a lithograph by J. D. Harding, London, 1822, in the Macpherson Collection.

[68] A BOAT GOING ON THE TAIL OF A FISH.

From a lithograph by J. D. Harding, London, 1822, in the Macpherson Collection.

[69] LANCING THE WHALE.
From a lithograph by J. D. Harding, London, 1822, in the Macpherson Collection.

[70] STRIKING A WHALE WITH THIRD HARPOON.
From a lithograph by J. D. Harding, London, 1822, in the Macpherson Collection.

[71] NORTHERN WHALE FISHERY — THE "HARMONY," OF HULL, AND OTHER WHALERS IN DAVIS STRAITS.

From a colored aquatint engraved by Duncan, after a painting by Huggins, 1829, in the Macpherson Collection.

[72] AN ENGLISH WHALER ROUNDING AN ICEBERG.
From a French lithograph, *ca.* 1835, in the Macpherson Collection.

[73] CUTTING IN THE WHALE.

From an engraving in de Page's "Voyage vers le Nord," Paris, n. d.

[74] DYING STRUGGLES OF THE SPERMACETI WHALE.
From "The Natural History of the Whale," Edinburgh, 1837.

[75] THE SPERMACETI WHALE OF THE SOUTHERN OCEAN.
From "The Natural History of the Whale," Edinburgh, 1837.

[76] "A SHOAL OF SPERM WHALES OFF THE ISLAND OF HAWAII IN WHICH THE SHIPS 'ENTERPRISE,' 'WM. ROACH,' 'POCAHONTAS' AND 'HOUQUA' WERE ENGAGED 10 DECR. 1833."

From a rare engraving by J. Hill (1838), after the painting by T. Birch, in the Allan Forbes Collection.

[77] VIEW OF NEW BEDFORD SHOWING THE "ORAZIMBO" AND "TARTERNO."

From a lithograph by Lane & Scott, 1845, in the Clark Collection, Massachusetts Institute of Technology.

[78] "CUTTING IN" A WHALE.

From an engraving by Rouarque (about 1850) in the Peabody Museum, Salem.

[79] PÊCHE DE LA BALEINE — WHALE FISHERY.

From a French aquatint, after Garneray, published about 1850, in the Macpherson Collection.

[80] PÊCHE DU CACHALOT — CACHALOT FISHING.
From a French aquatint, after Garneray, published about 1850, in the Macpherson Collection.

[81] THE WHALE FISHERY: ATTACKING A RIGHT WHALE AND CUTTING IN.

From a colored lithograph by Currier and Ives, copying a French aquatint, in the Clark Collection, Massachusetts Institute of Technology.

[82] THE WHALE FISHERY: SPERM WHALE "IN A FLURRY."
From a lithograph by Currier and Ives, in the Allan Forbes Collection.

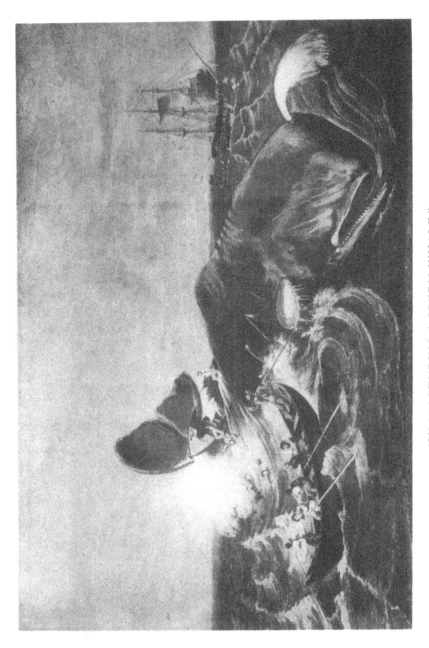

[83] "CAPTURING A SPERM WHALE."

From a colored engraving by J. Hill, after a painting by William Page, in the Allan Forbes Collection.

[84] THE WHALE FISHERY — "LAYING ON."

From a lithograph by N. Currier, New York, 1852, in the Allan Forbes Collection.

[85] THE WHALE FISHERY — "CAPTURING THE WHALE."
From a lithograph by N. Currier, New York, 1852, in the Allan Forbes Collection.

THE WHALE FISHERY IN A FLURRY.

[86] THE WHALE FISHERY — "IN A FLURRY."

From a lithograph by N. Currier, New York, 1852, in the Allan Forbes Collection.

[87] VIEW OF NEW BEDFORD FROM FAIR HAVEN IN 1853.

From an engraving by W. Wellstood, after a drawing by J. W. Hill, in the Allan Forbes Collection.

[88] SPERM WHALING, NO. 1 — "THE CHASE."

From a lithograph by Endicott & Co., New York, 1859, after drawings by A. Van Best and R. S. Gifford, corrected by Benjamin Russell, in the Allan Forbes Collection.

[89] SPERM WHALING, NO. 2 — "THE CONFLICT."

From a lithograph by Prang and Mayer, Boston, 1859, after a drawing by J. Cole, in the Allan Forbes Collection.

[126]

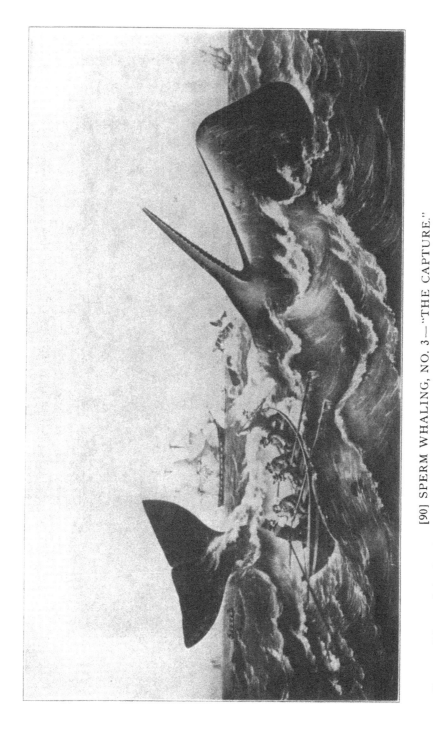

[90] SPERM WHALING, NO. 3—"THE CAPTURE."

From a lithograph by Endicott & Co., New York, 1862, after drawings by A. Van Best and R. S. Gifford, corrected by Benjamin Russell, in the Allan Forbes Collection.

[91] SCENE IN THE POLAR REGIONS.

From a colored lithograph, Paris, 1860, in the Macpherson Collection.

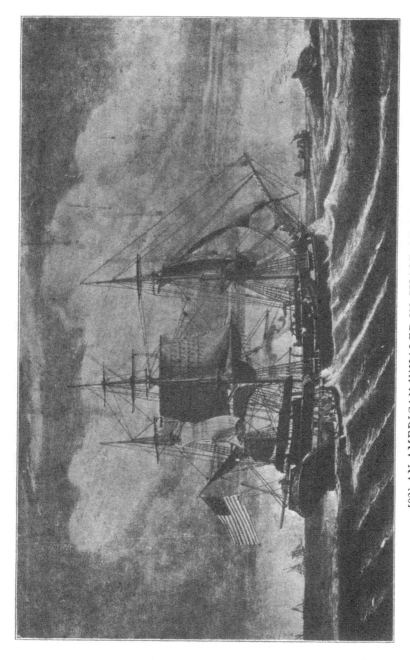

[92] AN AMERICAN WHALER IN CHASE OF A WHALE.

From a French lithograph, *ca.* 1860 (a copy of a Currier and Ives lithograph), in the Macpherson Collection.

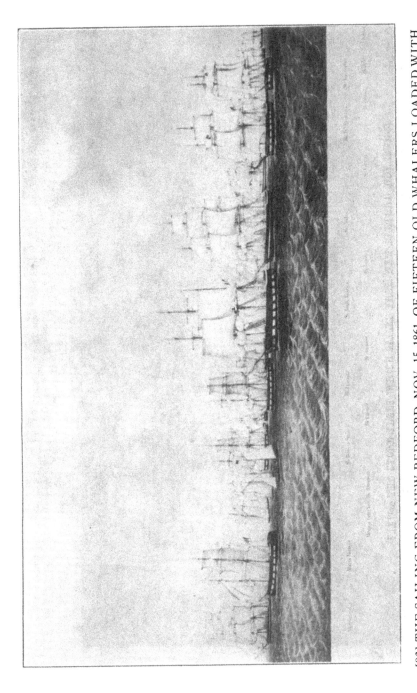

[93] THE SAILING FROM NEW BEDFORD, NOV. 15, 1861, OF FIFTEEN OLD WHALERS LOADED WITH STONES, TO BE SUNK IN THE CHANNELS OF THE HARBORS OF CHARLESTON AND SAVANNAH TO PREVENT BLOCKADE RUNNING.

From a lithograph by L. Prang & Co., 1862, in the Allan Forbes Collection.

[94] RIGHT WHALING IN BEHRING STRAITS, WITH ITS VARIETIES.

From a lithograph by J. H. Bufford (1871), after a drawing by Benjamin Russell, in the Allan Forbes Collection.

[95] SPERM WHALING AND ITS VARIETIES.

From a lithograph by J. H. Bufford (1871), after a drawing by Benjamin Russell, in the Allan Forbes Collection.

[96] SPERM WHALING — TAKING UP THE BOATS.
Lithograph, after a painting by Benjamin Russell, in the Allan Forbes Collection.

[97] ABANDONMENT OF THE WHALERS IN THE ARCTIC OCEAN, SEPTEMBER, 1871, NO. I.
From a lithograph by J. H. Bufford (1872), after a drawing by Benjamin Russell, in the Allan Forbes Collection.

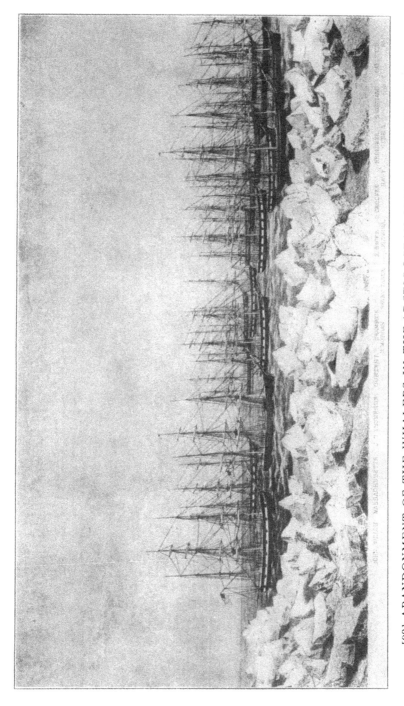

[98] ABANDONMENT OF THE WHALERS IN THE ARCTIC OCEAN, SEPTEMBER, 1871, NO. II.
From a lithograph by J. H. Bufford (1872), after a drawing by Benjamin Russell, in the Allan Forbes Collection.

[135]

[99] ABANDONMENT OF THE WHALERS IN THE ARCTIC OCEAN, SEPTEMBER, 1871, NO. III.
From a lithograph by J. H. Bufford (1872), after a drawing by Benjamin Russell, in the Allan Forbes Collection.

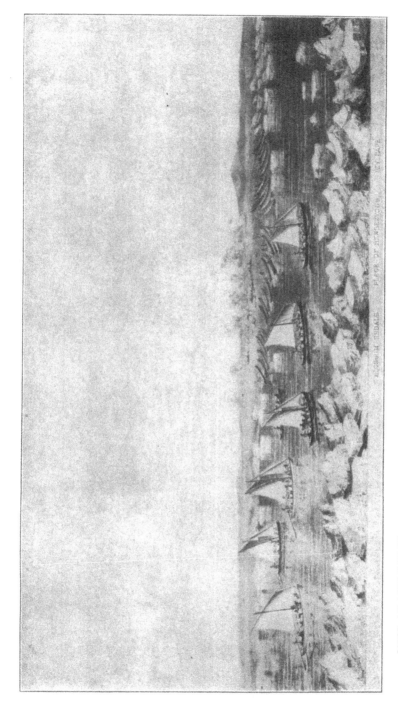

[100] ABANDONMENT OF THE WHALERS IN THE ARCTIC OCEAN, SEPTEMBER, 1871, NO. IV.
From a lithograph by J. H. Bufford (1872), after a drawing by Benjamin Russell, in the Allan Forbes Collection.

[101] ABANDONMENT OF THE WHALERS IN THE ARCTIC OCEAN, SEPTEMBER, 1871, NO. V.
From a lithograph by J. H. Bufford (1872), after a drawing by Benjamin Russell, in the Allan Forbes Collection.

[102] A FRENCH WHALER.

From the painting by François Roux, 1881, in the Musée de Marine du Louvre.

[103] THE BRITISH WHALERS "AMELIA WILSON" AND "CASTOR" OFF THE ISLAND OF BOURO, IN THE SOUTH SEA FISHERY.

From an aquatint, after a painting by W. J. Huggins, 1825, in the Clark Collection, Massachusetts Institute of Technology.

[104] WHALER "ANN ALEXANDER," OF NEW BEDFORD, ATTACKED BY A
WHALE IN 1850 AND SUNK IN A FEW MINUTES.

From a water-color in the possession of the Old Dartmouth Historical Society, New Bedford.

[105] BARK "CANTON," OF NEW BEDFORD, BUILT AT BALTIMORE IN 1835.

[106] BARK "CANTON PACKET," OF NEW BEDFORD, BUILT IN 1841.
Lost in a typhoon off Japan in 1867. From the painting in the Museum of the Old Dartmouth Historical Society.

[107] THE WHALE SHIP "CASTOR" ON HER VOYAGE TO THE SOUTH SEA FISHERY.
From an oil painting in the possession of Mess T. H. Parker, London.

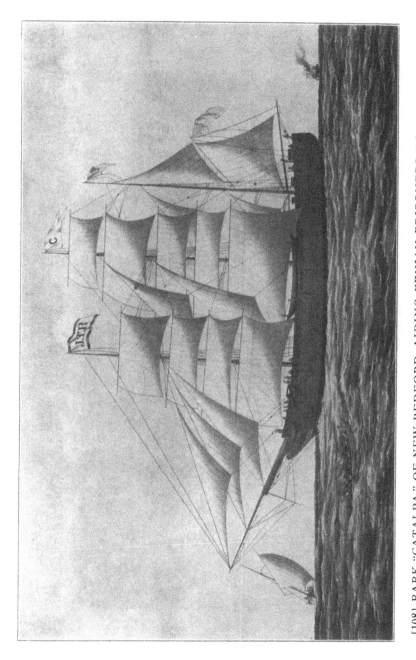

[108] BARK "CATALPA," OF NEW BEDFORD, AIDING FENIAN PRISONERS TO ESCAPE FROM AUSTRALIA.

From the colored lithograph by Forbes Lithograph Co. (1876), after the drawing by E. N. Russell, in the Allan Forbes Collection.

[109] WHALING BARK "COMMODORE MORRIS," OF NEW BEDFORD, BUILT IN 1841.
From a photograph in the Frank Wood Collection.

[110] BOW AND FIGUREHEAD OF THE BARK "COMMODORE MORRIS," OF NEW BEDFORD, BUILT IN 1841.

[111] WHALERS 'DESDEMONA,' 1823, AND "ROUSSEAU," 1801, DISMANTLED AT A
NEW BEDFORD WHARF

From a photograph made about 1895.

[112] SHIP "ELIZA ADAMS," OF NEW BEDFORD, BUILT IN 1835.

[113] WHALING SHIP "ELIZA ADAMS," 403 TONS,
BUILT AT FAIRHAVEN, MASS., IN 1835.
From a painting by C. S. Raleigh, in the Peabody Museum,
Salem.

[114] WHALING SHIP "GEORGE," OF NEW BEDFORD.
From a water-color painted at Havre by Montardier.

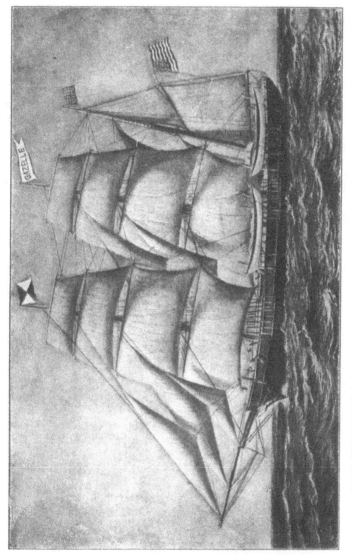

[115] WHALING BARK "GAZELLE," OF NEW BEDFORD, 340 TONS.

Altered from a ship about 1855.

[116] BARK "GEORGE AND SUSAN," OF NEW BEDFORD, BUILT IN 1810.

[117] WHALING BARK "JAMES ALLEN," OF NEW BEDFORD (AT RIGHT), WHALING
BARK "PLATINA," OF NEW BEDFORD (AT LEFT).

[118] WHALING BARK "JAMES ALLEN," OF NEW BEDFORD, BUILT
AT FAIRHAVEN IN 1844.

[119] A WHALING SHIP "HOVE DOWN" AT A NEW BEDFORD
WHARF.

[120] THE WHALING BRIG "JANE," AND THE CUTTER "BEAUFOY", FEB. 20, 1823, IN 74° 15′, SOUTH.

From a colored aquatint by W. J. Huggins, in the Macpherson Collection.

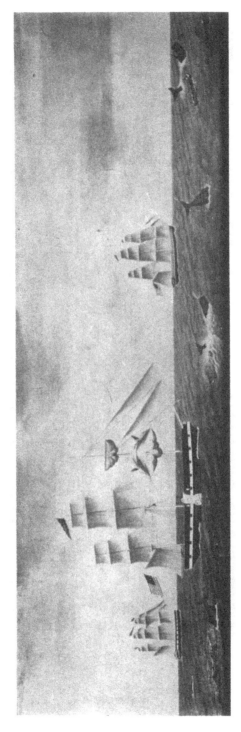

[121] WHALING SHIP "JULIAN," OF NEW BEDFORD, 356 TONS, BUILT AT DUXBURY IN 1828.
Half of a large oil painting in the Peabody Museum, Salem.

[122] WHALING BARK "KATHLEEN," OF NEW BEDFORD, BUILT IN 1844. ATTACKED BY A WHALE IN 1902 AND SUNK IN A FEW MINUTES.

From the oil painting by E. N. Russell, in the Allan Forbes Collection.

[123] WHALER "KUTUSOFF," OF NEW BEDFORD, 415 TONS, BUILT IN 1841.

[158]

[124] WHALER "KUTOSOFF," OF NEW BEDFORD, CUTTING IN HER LAST RIGHT WHALE ON THE NORTHWEST COAST.

From a lithograph by A. Mayer, Paris, after a drawing by Benjamin Russell, in the Allan Forbes Collection.

[125] BRIG "LEONORA," BUILT IN 1874, DRYING HER SAILS AT
A NEW BEDFORD WHARF.

[126] SHIP "MARIA," OF NEW BEDFORD, BUILT AT
PEMBROKE, MASS., IN 1782.

The oldest whaler in the United States in 1853.
From a wood engraving in the Allan Forbes Collection.

[127] WHALING BARK "MARS," OF NEW BEDFORD, 251 TONS, BUILT AT BOSTON IN 1825.

[128] WHALING BARK "MARS," OF NEW BEDFORD, 251 TONS, BUILT AT BOSTON IN 1825. View on deck looking forward, showing work bench and try-works in the center.

[129] WHALING BARK "MINNESOTA," OF NEW BEDFORD.
From a photograph made about 1876, in the Frank Wood Collection.

[130] WHALING BARK "MORNING STAR," OF NEW BEDFORD, BUILT IN 1858, DRYING HER SAILS AT A NEW BEDFORD WHARF.

[131] STEAM WHALER "ORCA," OF SAN FRANCISCO, CUTTING IN A RIGHT WHALE IN OCT., 1887, IN THE ARCTIC, DURING A SNOW STORM, SHOWING THE JAW WITH THE WHALEBONE BEING HAULED ON BOARD.

From a photograph in the Frank Wood Collection.

[132] WHALER "PHOENIX," OF WHITBY, ENGLAND, EMPLOYED IN THE GREENLAND
FISHERY, 1826-1833.

From a colored aquatint by Huggins, in the Macpherson Collection.

[133] WHALING BARK "PROGRESS," OF NEW BEDFORD, BUILT
AT WESTERLY, R. I., IN 1842.
Exhibited at the World's Fair, Chicago, 1893.

[134] BARK "PROGRESS," OF NEW BEDFORD, 340 TONS, BUILT
IN 1842.
A typical New Bedford whaler.

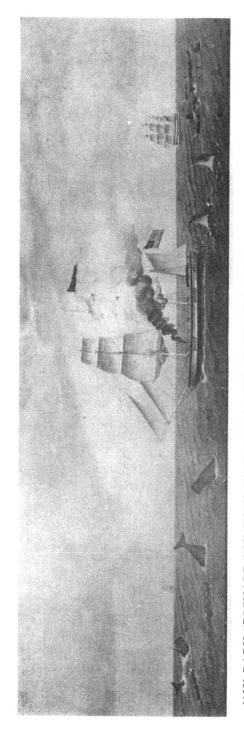

[135] BARK "RICHARD," 252 TONS, BUILT AT SALEM IN 1826, WHALING IN THE SOUTH PACIFIC IN 1837.
Part of a painting in the Peabody Museum, Salem.

[136] TWO OLD WHALERS AT A NEW BEDFORD WHARF.
Ship "Rousseau," 305 tons (1801), and ship "Desdemona," 236 tons
(1823).

[137] WHALING BARK "COMMODORE MORRIS," 355 TONS,
DISMANTLED AT A NEW BEDFORD WHARF.

[138] OLD WHALERS LYING AT A NEW BEDFORD WHARF.

The ship "Rousseau," 305 tons, built at Philadelphia in 1801; and the ship "Desdemona," 236 tons, built at Middletown, Conn., in 1823.

[139] SHIP "SALLY ANNE," OF BOSTON, 312 TONS, BUILT AT BRAINTREE IN 1804.
Became a New Bedford whaler in 1846 and was wrecked on the Friendly Islands, Apr. 2, 1854.

[140] WHALE SHIP "SAMUEL ENDERBY," OF LONDON, BUILT IN 1834, BOUND IN FROM THE SOUTH SEA FISHERY.

From a colored lithograph, after a painting by W. J. Huggins, 1834, in the Macpherson Collection.

[141] WHALER "SPLENDID," AT NEW ZEALAND, 1912.
From a photograph in the Peabody Museum, Salem.

[142] WHALING BARK "TAMERLANE," OF NEW BEDFORD, BUILT
AT WISCASSET, ME., IN 1824.
From a photograph made in August, 1873, now in the collection of the Peabody
Museum, Salem.

[143] HERMAPHRODITE BRIG "VIOLA," OF PORTLAND,
MAINE, 139 TONS, BUILT AT ESSEX, MASS., IN 1910.

[144] THE DECK OF THE WHALER "VIOLA," OF PORTLAND,
MAINE.

[145] HERMAPHRODITE BRIG "VIOLA," OF PORTLAND, ME., BUILT IN 1910, WHALING OFF THE AFRICAN COAST.

[146] OLD WHALING VESSELS AT A NEW BEDFORD WHARF IN 1880.

From left to right:— Schooner "Antarctic," ships "Swallow," Desdemona," "Rousseau," and "Jireh Perry."

[147] A WHALER BEING "HOVE DOWN" AT A NEW BEDFORD WHARF.

From a photograph in the Frank Wood Collection.

[148] A "HOVE DOWN" WHALER AT A NEW BEDFORD WHARF.
From a photograph in the Frank Wood Collection.

[149] WHALING BARKS DRYING THEIR SAILS AT A NEW
BEDFORD WHARF.

[150] A WHALER "HOVE DOWN" AT A NEW BEDFORD WHARF IN 1882.

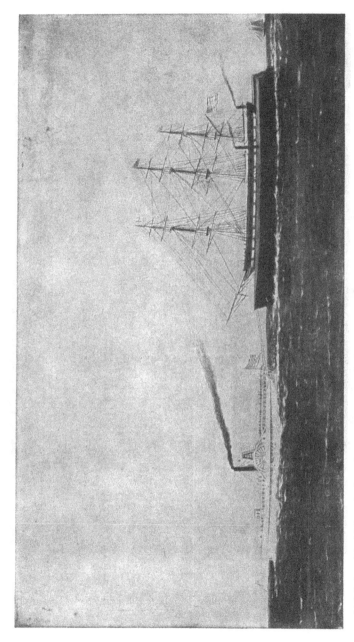

[151] A "CAMEL" FLOATING A WHALER TO SEA OVER THE NANTUCKET BAR (1842-1849).

From an engraving in the Allan Forbes Collection.

[152] WHALER "LAGODA," OF NEW BEDFORD.
The half-size model in the Bourne Whaling Museum, New Bedford.

THE WHALER "CHARLES W. MORGAN" OF NEW BEDFORD

THE whaler "Charles W. Morgan" was built at New Bedford in 1841. For her first seven voyages she was rigged as a ship and registered 351 tons. In 1867 she was re-rigged as a bark and her measured tonnage was then reduced to 313.75. At that time her hull measurements were: length, 105.6; breadth, 27.7; depth, 17.6.

This whaler was always a successful ship, never meeting with disaster and usually returning home with a good lay for all hands. She rounded Cape Horn many times, went whaling to the Arctic and Indian Oceans as well as the Atlantic and Pacific and also spent a season at Desolation in the Southern Indian Ocean.

Most of her voyages were made to the Pacific Ocean. Her ninth voyage, while under the command of Capt. John M. Tinkham, was made to the Indian Ocean and the next voyage, in 1875, was to the South Atlantic. Charles W. Morgan of New Bedford, her first owner, managed her for two voyages. She then passed into the control of Edward M. Robinson for one voyage and then for ten years was sent out by Mess. I. Howland, Jr. & Co. In 1863 she passed into the hands of Mess. J. & W. R. Wing who were her managing owners for fifty-three years.

This vessel was always employed in the whaling business and when built was constructed of the best materials and all copper fastened. When in need she was always promptly repaired which explains her good condition at the present time. Of her total number of thirty-seven voyages, twenty-two were made in part to Arctic or Antarctic waters where her hull was free from the attacks of worms. Between 1886 and 1904 she made yearly voyages out of San Francisco to Japan and the Okhotsk Sea and then returned to New Bedford after an absence of nearly twenty years. In 1916 she sailed for the Kergulen, or Desolation islands, in the Southern Indian Ocean, after sea elephant oil, and afterwards made three voyages to the Atlantic Ocean grounds. Her last arrival in New Bedford was in 1921.

The luck of the "Morgan" was not due to any one captain for there was a change of commanders nearly every voyage. Captain Norton was her first commander and after an absence of three years and four months he returned with 2400 barrels of oil in her hold. Her second voyage was under Captain Sampson who was married just before he sailed and took with him his young bride. It was three years and six months before she again saw New Bedford. Such an experience must have been a severe test for the affection and endurance of any woman. The whaler brought home 2270 barrels of oil. Her most successful voyage seems to have been under Captain James A. Hamilton, who escaped storm, lee shore and Confederate cruiser and returned to New Bedford, May 12, 1863, bringing 1935 barrels of oil, having also previously sent home 2280 barrels. At prevailing war-time prices the profits of this voyage must have been considerable. The "Morgan" was usually away from home three years and five months. Her outfitting generally required five months' time.

As the price of oil fell lower and lower the time came when it was no longer profitable to send out whale ships and the "Charles W. Morgan," after her return in 1921, was dismantled. Late that year her shares were purchased by Mr. Harry Neyland, the artist, and other members of the New Bedford Whaling Club, with the intention of preserving her and also using her as the headquarters of the Club. After this she was used on two occasions by moving picture companies. The first filming of the "Morgan" occurred when with the whaler "Wanderer" (since wrecked on Cuttyhunk in the gale of August 26, 1924) she was used in "Down to the Sea in Ships" — a very successful production and a splendid picture. Subsequently she figured in the screen version of Hergesheimer's "Java Head."

But she has now reached her last port and her hull rests in a stone cradle beside a wharf at South Dartmouth, Mass., ten miles below New Bedford and barely a stone's throw from the spot where Bartholomew Gosnold landed in May, 1603. There she is to be preserved for so long as her timbers shall last. Mr. Neyland having purchased twenty-eight of the thirty-two shares in the "Charles W. Morgan" and having failed to interest the City of New Bedford in the preservation of the whaler, then turned to Col. E. H. R. Green, a descendant of an early owner, and through his interest and munificence she has been acquired, refitted and opened to the public as a living monument to the New Bedford whale fishery. Near at hand a whaling museum is to be erected and with ample endowment "Whaling Enshrined, Inc." will preserve and visualize for posterity the last of the old-time whalers and also every sort of implement and equipment used in an industry that has seen its day and is no more.

[153] WHALER "CHARLES W. MORGAN," OF NEW BEDFORD, 314
TONS, BUILT AT NEW BEDFORD IN 1841.

[154] WHALER "CHARLES W. MORGAN," OF NEW BEDFORD.

[155] WHALER "CHARLES W. MORGAN," OF NEW BEDFORD.

[156] WHALER "CHARLES W. MORGAN," OF NEW BEDFORD.

[157] WHALER "CHARLES W. MORGAN," OF NEW BEDFORD.

[158] WHALER "CHARLES W. MORGAN," OF NEW BEDFORD.
Showing the stone and cement cradle in which the ship now rests.

[159] WHALER "CHARLES W. MORGAN," OF NEW BEDFORD.

Showing the stone and cement cradle in which the ship now rests.

[160] WHALER "CHARLES W. MORGAN," OF NEW BEDFORD.

[161] WHALER "CHARLES W. MORGAN," OF NEW BEDFORD.
Looking up the mizzen-mast from the after deck-house.

[162] WHALER "CHARLES W. MORGAN," OF NEW BEDFORD.

After boat on the starboard side.

[163] WHALER "CHARLES W. MORGAN," OF NEW BEDFORD.
Showing the present gangway and the "cutting in" stage hoisted above it.

[164] WHALER "CHARLES W. MORGAN," OF NEW BEDFORD.
Looking from the after deck-house into a fully equipped whale boat.

[165] WHALER "CHARLES W. MORGAN," OF NEW BEDFORD.
Looking forward from the after deck-house, showing a "stove" boat on the deck-
house and the huge blocks and chains of the "cutting in" tackle
hanging from the cross-trees of the mainmast.

[166] WHALER "CHARLES W. MORGAN," OF NEW BEDFORD.
Looking aft, showing two boats on the deck-house that were "stove" by whales. The grindstone
is on the deck, at the right.

[167] WHALER "CHARLES W. MORGAN," OF NEW BEDFORD.

Looking forward, showing ropes coiled about the mainmast and the work bench and try-works at the right.

[168] WHALER "CHARLES W. MORGAN," OF NEW BEDFORD.

Showing the forecastle companion, windlass, ship's bell, windlass brake and three of the crew lowering sails.

[169] WHALER "CHARLES W. MORGAN," OF NEW BEDFORD.

Looking forward, showing the forecastle companion, windlass, ship's bell and windlass brake.

[170] WHALER "CHARLES W. MORGAN," OF NEW BEDFORD.
The wheel, and double-card compass inside the cabin skylight.

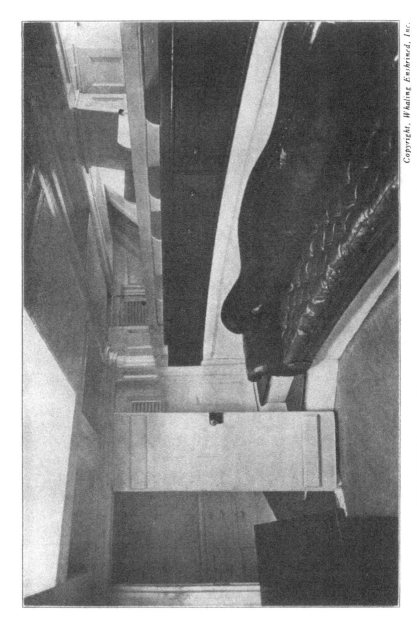

[171] WHALER "CHARLES W. MORGAN," OF NEW BEDFORD.

The captain's cabin.

[172] WHALER "CHARLES W. MORGAN," OF NEW BEDFORD.

The mates' cabin or mess room, showing the 1st mate's stateroom (at the left)
and the cook's pantry (at the right).

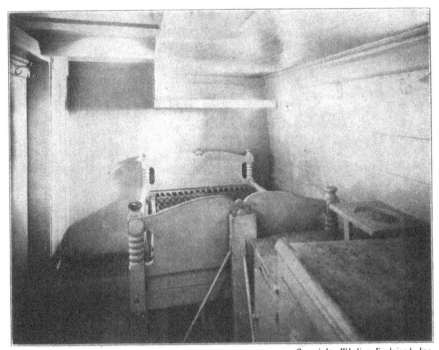

[173] WHALER "CHARLES W. MORGAN," OF NEW BEDFORD.
The captain's stateroom.

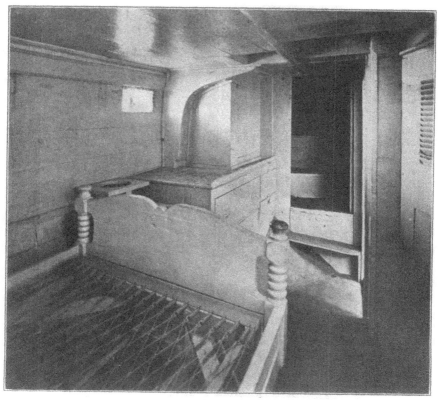

[174] WHALER "CHARLES W. MORGAN," OF NEW BEDFORD.
The captain's stateroom, showing at the rear his privy.

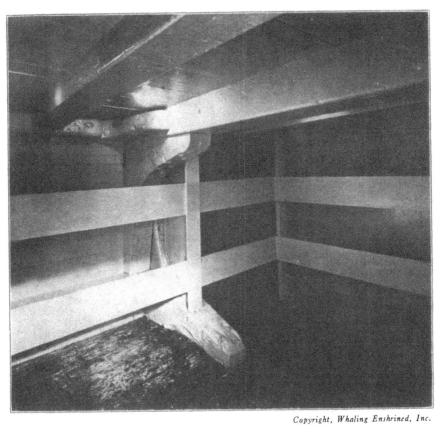

[175] WHALER "CHARLES W. MORGAN," OF NEW BEDFORD.
Bunks in the steerage for the harpooners.

[176] WHALER "CHARLES W. MORGAN," OF NEW BEDFORD.
The forecastle, showing the bunks for the whalemen.

[177] WHALER "CHARLES W. MORGAN," OF NEW BEDFORD.
The fresh-water tank forward between decks and below, an oil cask in the lower
main hold.

[178] WHALE OIL CASKS (COVERED WITH SEAWEED), FRESH-WATER TANKS, AND JUNK LYING ON THE DOCK.

[179] THE WHALING BRIG "LEONORA," OF NEW BEDFORD, AND
THE WHALING SHIP "CHARLES W. MORGAN," OF NEW
BEDFORD, 314 TONS, BUILT AT NEW BEDFORD IN 1841.
From a photograph made about 1900.

[180] THE WHALE THAT CAME ASHORE AT SCHEVENINGEN, HOLLAND, IN 1598.
From a colored engraving by Van der Gouwen, in the Allan Forbes Collection.

[181] THE WHALE THAT CAME ASHORE JAN. 13, 1610, AT BEUER, HOLLAND.
From an engraving by John Fansson, 1618, in the Allan Forbes Collection.

Effigie del Pesce comunemente chiamato BALENOTTO, il quale sotto li 18. Aprile 1715. fu dalla Barca condotta da Padron Domenico Cavalieri fermato poco lungi dal Porto di questa Città con gran colo laccio. Il medesimo era di lunghezza piedi 48., e di grossezza 26. La Mascella di sotto, la quale solamente era munita di denti in numero di 48., s'estendeva 2 piedi undici, e due terzi per lungo, e la di lei apertura inferiore verso la Testa a piedi quattro, e due terzi. Aveva la Coda nel fine grossa piedi tre, e larga piedi 11. L'occhio appariva tagliato all'uso di quello del Porco, e grande un piede. Gettava dalle narici acqua in gran coppia, e a considerabile altezza, essendo la medema lunga d'in circa piedi due. Il peso poi di tutto il sudetto Pesce montava a libre cento venti, e più milla. La Fune con cui fu questi assalito, e legato dal detto Padron Domenico, con una scossa di coda, subitamente l'infranse, e di nuovo assicurato con raddoppiati canapi faceva tanta violenza, che quantunque la Barca veleggiasse con vento favorevole, la tirava per la parte contraria con sommo stupore de' Marinari, ma li convenne poi cedere a più colpi di Brandistocchi, mentre a nulla servivano le archibuggiate, e della prodigiosa quantità del Sangue uscitogli dalle molte ferite, restò finalmente nel termine d'ore dodici svenato, & ucciso. Fattosi in appresso in più pezzi il suo Corpo, si è ricavato dal solo Grasso 80., e più Somme d'Oglio, & ora il suo Teschio, e Mascella dentata si trovano in Casa del Padron Viola, Testimonj Veraci d'una Preda così portentosa.

In PESARO, Per gli Eredi di Demetrio Degni Stamp. Cam & Ep.

MDCCXV. CON LICENZA DE' SUPERIORI.

[182] WHALING SCENE IN 1715.
From an Italian broadside in the Allan Forbes Collection.

[183] THE WHALE STRANDED AT ZANTVOORD, HOLLAND, FEB. 2, 1762.

From a colored engraving in the Allan Forbes Collection.

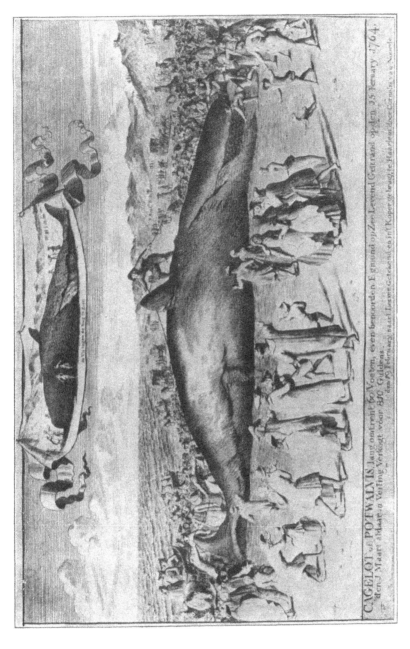

[184] THE WHALE STRANDED AT EGMOND, HOLLAND, FEB. 15, 1764.

From an engraving in the Allan Forbes Collection.

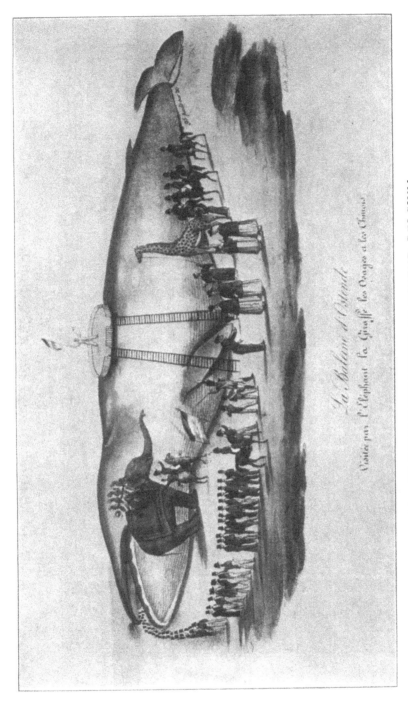

La Baleine d'Ostende

Vendue par l'Elephant la Giraffe les Oranges et les Citrons

[185] THE WHALE STRANDED AT OSTEND, BELGIUM.

From a colored lithograph by Langlume, designed to show the comparative size of the larger mammals, in the Allan Forbes Collection.

[186] JAPANESE PICNICKERS VIEWING WHALES IN
SHINAGAWA BAY.
From a Japanese print by Katsukawa (1770-1820) in the Allan Forbes Collection.

[187] CAPTURING A "SPOUTER," OFF ZANZIBAR.
From an engraving by Jazet, after L. Garneray, in the Allan Forbes Collection.

[188] CUTTING OFF FROM A STAGE, THE CASE, OR HEAD, OF A
SPERM WHALE.
From a photograph made in 1903. Courtesy of Mess. H. S. Hutchinson & Co.,
New Bedford, Mass.

[189] JUNK COMING IN AT THE WAIST.
From a photograph made in 1903. Courtesy of Mess. H. S. Hutchinson & Co.,
New Bedford, Mass.

[190] "CUTTING IN," SHOWING BLUBBER BEING STRIPPED FROM
THE WHALE.

From a photograph made in 1903. Courtesy of Mess. H. S. Hutchinson & Co.,
New Bedford, Mass.

[191] HOISTING IN THE LOWER JAW OF A SPERM WHALE.
From a photograph made in 1903. Courtesy of Mess. H. S. Hutchinson & Co.,
New Bedford, Mass.

[192] BUILDING "TRY WORKS" ON THE SCHOONER "A. V. WOODRUFF," OF NEW BEDFORD.

[193] "TRY WORKS" COVERED WITH A TARPAULIN.

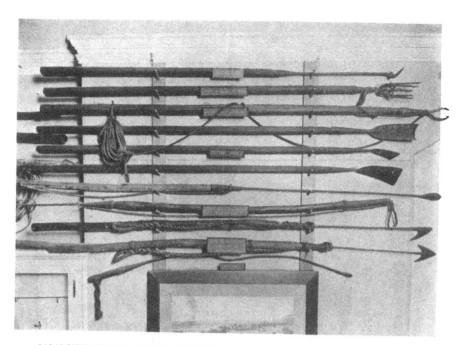

[194] WHALING IMPLEMENTS, MOUNTED READY FOR USE.
From above: blubber fork; grains (2), for handling blubber; cutting spades (3); lances, for killing whales at close quarters (2); single and two-flued harpoons, old type; head needle; in the Peabody Museum, Salem.

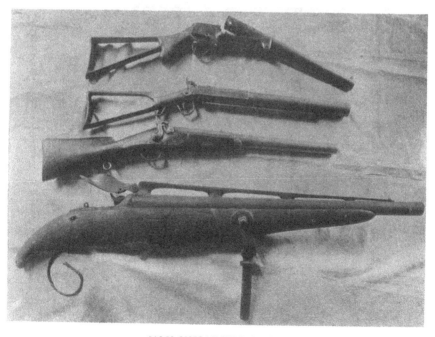

[195] WHALING GUNS.
From above: brass, breech-loading, bomb-lance shoulder gun; two forms of muzzle-loading, bomb-lance shoulder guns; Greener harpoon gun; in the Peabody Museum, Salem.

[196] DISMANTLED "TRY KETTLES" BESIDE A NEW BEDFORD WAREHOUSE.
From a photograph made about 1910.

[197] IMPLEMENTS BELONGING TO A WHALE BOAT.

1. Oar 2. Boat-waif 3. Boat-hook 4. Paddle 5. Boat Sails 6. Sweeping-line-buoy
7. Lead to Sweeping-line 8. Cock-pin 9. Short-warp 10. Boat-piggin 11. Boat-keg
12. Lantern-key 13. Sweeping-line 14. Boat-hatchet 15. Lance-warp 16. Boat-grapnel
17. Boat-knife 18. Fog-horn 19. Line-tub 20. Bcat-bucket 21. Drag 22. Nipper 23.
Boat-crotch 24. Boat-compass 25. Boat-anchor 26. Row-lock 27. Tub-oar-crotch.

From Scammon's "Marine Mammals," San Francisco, 1874.

[229]

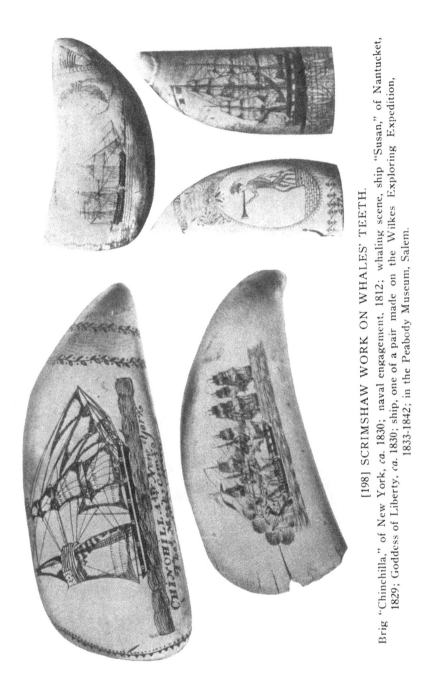

[198] SCRIMSHAW WORK ON WHALES' TEETH.

Brig "Chinchilla," of New York, *ca.* 1830; naval engagement, 1812; whaling scene, ship "Susan," of Nantucket, 1829; Goddess of Liberty, *ca.* 1830; ship, one of a pair made on the Wilkes Exploring Expedition, 1833-1842; in the Peabody Museum, Salem.

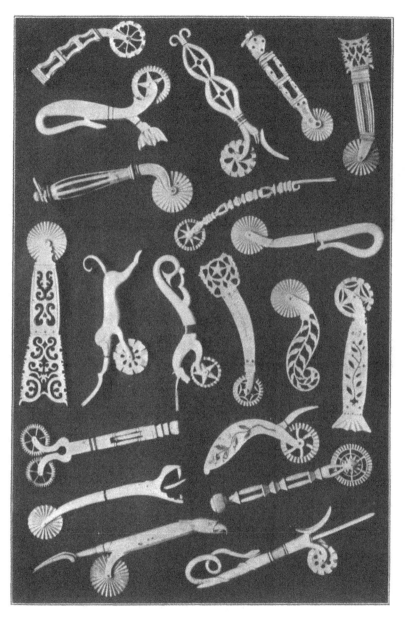

[199] "JAGGING WHEELS," MADE OF WHALE IVORY BY NEW BEDFORD WHALEMEN, USED TO CRIMP PASTRY ROUND THE EDGE OF A PIE.

From the Frank Wood Collection.

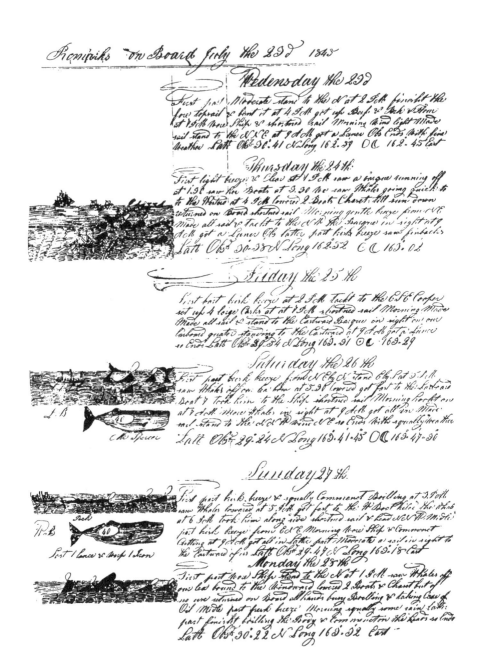

[200] A PAGE FROM THE LOG OF THE SHIP "FRANCES," OF NEW BEDFORD, WHALING OFF JAPAN IN 1845.

IN MEMORY OF
ELI DODGE,
WHO WAS KILLED BY A WHALE,

Sept. 4, 1858, off the Coast of New Holland.

COMPOSED AT SEA,

BY HENRY GOODING.

He has gone from our gaze, he'll never more return,
A shipmate we all did revere,
We no more of him, our duty will learn,
No more with us, will he make cheer.

He had perhaps a dear cottage home,
Or maybe a sister or a brother,
Who knows but a wife,
The joy of his life.
A child, or a fond loving mother.

He was brave in the storm,
He was kind in the calm,
His duty he done like a man,
But now he is free from this world's alarms,
And safe moor'd in the Spirit land.

He ofttimes with us did the monster pursue,
The huge monster king of the deep,
But now he is gone, and his journey is through,
Where loud billow's roll he does sleep.

How little we thought, but a moment before,
When near us he bravely did contend,
With the huge monster then weltering in its gore.
That he would to hades Eli send.

But he's gone from our gaze, his long race is run,
In death's cold embrace he does lie,
Yet Father of Mercies Thy will be done,
And take his soul to Thee on High.

[201] From the original in the Peabody Museum, Salem.

[202] "A DEAD WHALE OR A STOVE BOAT."
The Whalemen's Monument, by Bela L. Pratt, beside the entrance to
the New Bedford Public Library.

[203] A WHALING SCENE IN ANCIENT DAYS.
From an early engraving in the Allan Forbes Collection.

[204] JONAH SWALLOWED BY THE WHALE AND HIS
SUBSEQUENT ESCAPE.
From an early Dutch engraving in the Allan Forbes Collection.

EVOMIT ABSORPTVM CÆCO DE GVTTVRE CÆTVS,
REDDITVR ET TERRÆ QVI MODO PRÆDA FVIT.

M. de Vos inu .   Ant. Wierx fculp ,   I. Baptista Vrints excud .

[205] JONAH CAST UP BY THE WHALE.
From an engraving by Antoine Wierx in the Allan Forbes Collection.

[206] JONAH CAST UP BY THE WHALE.
From an engraving by Joan Sadler in the Allan Forbes Collection.

[207] JONAH CAST OVER BOARD.
From an old English engraving in the Allan Forbes Collection.

INDEX

Abandonment of the whalers in the Arctic in 1871, 134-138.
Adams, John, 35.
Amelia Wilson *(ship)*, 140.
Ann Alexander *(ship)*, 141.
Arctic regions, map of, 55.
Atkins, Captain, 27.

Barnstable (Mass.), 30.
Beaufoy *(cutter)*, 155.
Behring Straits fishery, 131.
Bellomont, Governor, 16.
Boston (Mass.), 35.
Bristol (R. I.), 31.
Brown, Obadiah, 36.
Browne & Co., Obadiah, 38.

"Camel," floating a whaler, 183.
Candle works, 36.
Candles, 35.
Canton *(bark)*, 142.
Canton Packet *(bark)*, 143.
Cape Cod, 6, 9.
Castor *(ship)*, 144.
Catalpa *(bark)*, 145.
Chadder, William, 25.
Champlain, Samuel de, 3.
Charles W. Morgan *(ship)*, 185-212.
Chinchilla *(brig)*, 232.
Clark, Captain, 29.
Coffin, Elisha, 22, 23.
Collins & Rivera, 39.
Commodore Morris *(bark)*, 146, 147, 170.
Crabb, Benjamin, 35.
Cranch, Richard, 36.

Cranch & Co., Richard, 38, 39.
Cranston, Samuel, 5.
Cutting in a whale, 110, 115, 222-225.

Daggett, Thomas, 20.
Davis, John, 30.
Davis Straits and Northern fishery, 27-29, 80, 96, 108.
Deborah Gifford *(ship), frontispiece.*
Desdemona *(bark)*, 148, 170, 171, 178.
Dodge, Eli, killed by whale, 233.
Drift whales, 9, 10, 15, 20.
Dunfee, Sarah L., viii.
Dutch whalers, 46-52, 56, 57, 61, 80, 85-89, 93, 94.

Eastham (Mass.), 9, 21.
Easthampton (N.Y.), 12, 15.
Edds, William, 21.
Eldridge, Nicholas, 21.
Eliza Adams *(ship)*, 149, 150.
Enterprise *(ship)*, 113.

Forbes, Allan, vii.
Fortune *(sloop)*, 33.
Frances *(ship)*, 232.
French whaler, 139.

Gazelle *(bark)*, 151.
George *(ship)*, 150.
George and Susan *(bark)*, 152.
Gosnold, Bartholomew, 187.
Green, Col. E. H. R., viii, 187.
Greenland fishery, 27-29, 63-65, 67-97.